Cute and Simple
Woodworking

35 BEAUTIFUL STEP-BY-STEP
PROJECTS FOR THE HOME

Jennifer Burt with *Joanna Teague*

CICO BOOKS

LONDON NEW YORK

This book is dedicated to all women who love making things and have a passion for craft of whatever kind.

Published in 2013 by CICO Books
An imprint of Ryland Peters & Small
519 Broadway, 5th Floor, New York NY 10012
20–21 Jockey's Fields, London WC1R 4BW
www.rylandpeters.com

10 9 8 7 6 5 4 3 2 1

A CIP catalog record for this book is available from the Library of Congress and the British Library.

ISBN: 978-1-78249-050-0

Printed in China

Editor: Sarah Hoggett
Designer: Geoff Borin
Illustrator: Stephen Dew
Photographer: Caroline Arber
Stylist: Nel Haynes

Cute and Simple
Woodworking

CONTENTS

INTRODUCTION

Woodwork is a highly enjoyable craft and has many facets. I have written this book to show how it can be used to make beautiful things to use around the home and to give as special gifts. If you are new to woodworking, take the time to read through the Woodworking Know-how section (see page 119) to learn some of the basics about handling wood as a material and the kind of tools you will need.

Some of the projects are simple pieces that are perfect for involving the children in decorating; others are more complicated and will take longer to complete. Each project has a skill level at the start, so use that as a guide. Take your time and enjoy the process: you will produce things that are both useful and beautiful. You can easily adapt the projects by changing the finish to match your décor, or use the decorative techniques to upcycle other wooden items and furniture that you already have.

As well as standard woodworking techniques, I also have included methods that I have learned through experimenting over the years. I love combining woodworking with other crafts, such as sewing, to add texture and interest.

Wood is such a versatile and readily available material that is loved by many people. It amazes me that I can start with a piece of wood and a few tools and, within a couple of hours, have created something to treasure for years. I hope that you will learn to love woodwork as much as I do and that this book will inspire you to use it to produce gifts for friends and family and objects for your own home, while enjoying the process of learning a new skill.

CHAPTER 1

HALLWAY AND LIVING ROOM

As you work through the projects in this chapter, you will learn some of the very basics of woodwork. I remember how rewarding it was when I first started working with wood—as I cut my first simple shape and turned a small bit of wood into an object that I could put on display. Why not start out with making the boot holder (page 31)? The technique is simple, but you can decorate the boot holder however you choose so it provides the perfect way of adding a splash of color to your home.

Rustic BIRD AND HEART

Add a touch of love to your home with hearts and birds, perfect for hanging on door handles, drawer knobs, and drape tie-backs, or in your hallway to welcome people as they walk in. As a variation, try making your own heart templates and painting them with other paint techniques in different colors.

YOU WILL NEED:

Materials

Templates on page 138

Planed pine, ¼–½ in. (6–12 mm) thick and at least 2¾ in. (70 mm) wide

Water-based paint in two colors

Latex-based adhesive

String or ribbon

Equipment

Tracing paper and pencil

Clamps

Workbench

Coping saw

Drill and ⁹⁄₆₄-in. (3.5-mm) drill bit

Coarse and fine sandpaper

Dust mask

Paintbrushes

1 Trace the bird and heart templates on page 138, cut out, and draw around them on the wood, taking the grain of the wood into account. Mark where the hanging holes are to be drilled.

2 Securely clamp the wood to the workbench. Using a coping saw, cut out the wood shapes (see page 121); you may need to re-clamp the pieces as you cut around them. Drill the hanging holes using a ⁹⁄₆₄-in. (3.5-mm) bit.

3 Sand the bird and heart, then rub the pieces with an old cloth to remove any dust (see page 131).

4 Paint each piece with your chosen base color. Depending on the color and quality of the paint, you may need to apply two or three coats (see page 131). Randomly dab latex-based adhesive along the edges and on the surface of the heart and bird (see page 132). Once the adhesive has dried, apply your chosen top coat; again, you may need to apply several coats.

5 Using fine sandpaper, rub gently over the bird and heart. As you rub, the latex under the top coat will come away, revealing the base color. (Don't rub too hard or you will sand right back down to the wood.)

6 Check the holes for the hanging threads: if they are blocked with paint, scrape them out with a wooden toothpick. Push the string or ribbon through the holes, using a twisting action. Make a loose knot halfway up the string and give the piece a tug down. Tie the loose ends together in an overhand knot.

IN STEP 2, PLACE THE POINT OF THE HEART AND THE BEAK OF THE BIRD NEAR THE EDGE OF THE WOOD TO SAVE ENERGY SAWING.

Key HOOKS

I love designing and making useful things for my home and this key hook is one of them. It's simple and can be made in no time at all—but once in place, it will last a lifetime. Like all the projects in this book, you can paint it in colors that coordinate with your room. I have chosen hooks that have been hand forged, but as long as they are the right size, any small hooks will do.

YOU WILL NEED:

Materials

Templates on page 137

Planed pine, 16 x 4¾ x ¾–1 in. (400 x 120 x 18–25 mm), for the key hook

Planed pine, 8 x 4 x 5⁄16 in. (200 x 100 x 6–8 mm), for the heart

Water-based paint in your chosen color

Wood glue

Three decorative hooks, approx. 1½ in. (35 mm) long

Equipment

Tracing paper and pencil

Clamps

Workbench

Coping saw

Electric jigsaw (optional)

Dust mask

Safety goggles

Coarse and fine sandpaper

Wood glue

Paintbrush

Bradawl

Small slotted (flat-headed) screwdriver

1 Trace the key-hook template on page 137, cut out, and draw around it on the wood, taking the grain of the wood into account. Repeat with the small heart template.

2 Securely clamp the wood for the key rack to the workbench. Cut out the wood shape. You may prefer to use an electric jigsaw rather than a coping saw; see page 121. Whichever tool you choose, you will need to re-clamp often to maneuver the saw around the cutting line and the clamps. Securely clamp the heart piece to the workbench and cut it out using a coping saw. (For a piece this size, it is too dangerous to use an electric jigsaw.)

3 Sand the key hook and heart, then rub the pieces with an old cloth to remove any dust (see page 131).

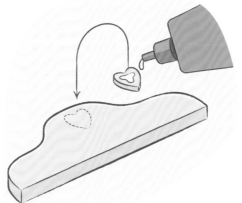

4 Apply a little glue to the back of the heart and glue it to the key hook, using the template as a guide. Wipe off any excess glue.

5 Paint the key hook and heart in your chosen color. Depending on the quality of the paint, you may need to apply two or three coats (see page 131).

6 Place the template on the front of the key rack. Push the bradawl through the template at the marked points; this is where the hooks will be attached. Remove the template, then use the bradawl to make a pilot hole (see page 127) at each marked point. Attach the hooks using a slotted (flat-headed) screwdriver.

7 Attach the key rack to the wall, following the instructions on page 133.

Bird WITH FABRIC WINGS

This pretty little rustic bird is always popular with adults and children alike. The combination of fabric and wood is unusual and friends will be amazed that you have sewn through wood. Hang it on the end of the bed to give your child "tweet" dreams!

YOU WILL NEED:

Materials

Template on page 138

Planed pine, 12 x 3½ x ⁵⁄₁₆ in. (300 x 80 x 7–8 mm); a 12-in./30-cm length of tongue-and-groove paneling is ideal

Water-based paints in your chosen colors for the body, beak, and eye

Scraps of pretty fabric

Sewing thread and needle

Small amount of polyester toy filling

Approx. 15 in. (38 cm) string or ribbon for hanging

Equipment

Tracing paper, pencil, and paper

Clamps

Workbench

Coping saw

Dust mask

Safety goggles

Drill and ⁵⁄₆₄- and ⁹⁄₆₄-in. (2- and 3.5-mm) drill bits

Coarse and fine sandpaper

Small and very fine paintbrushes

Wooden toothpick

Scissors

1 Trace the bird template on page 138, cut out, and draw around it on the wood, taking the grain of the wood into account.

2 Securely clamp the wood to the workbench. Using a coping saw, cut out the bird (see page 121); you may need to re-clamp the piece as you cut around it. Using the template, mark where the hanging hole is to be drilled. (The wing holes will be drilled after painting.) Drill the hole using a ⁹⁄₆₄-in. (3.5-mm) bit.

3 Sand the bird, then rub the piece with an old cloth to remove any dust (see page 131).

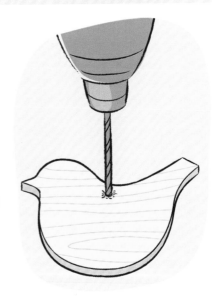

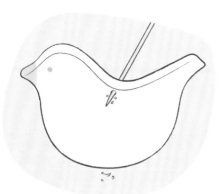

4 Paint the body of the bird. Depending on the quality of the paint, you may need to apply two or three coats (see page 131). Carefully add the details of the beak and the eye, using the template as a reference. Leave to dry. Check the hole for the hanging thread: if it is blocked with paint, scrape it out with a wooden toothpick.

5 Using the template, mark the position of the wing holes. Drill the holes using a ⁵⁄₆₄-in. (2-mm) bit.

6 Trace the wing template on page 138 onto paper, cut out, and pin to the fabric. Cut two shapes for the front of the wing and two for the back, remembering to reverse the template for the back wing pieces. Place one front and one back wing wrong sides together. Using a contrasting color of thread, work a line of tiny running stitches approx. ⅛ in. (3 mm) from the edge, leaving a small gap for stuffing. Fill the wing with a little polyester toy filling and sew up the hole. Repeat for the other wing.

7 Thread a needle with strong sewing thread, take the needle through one wing hole and then through the other hole in the bird, leaving plenty of thread to tie the final knot. Place one wing in position on the front of the bird. Bring the needle up though the bird into the first wing hole and pull tight. Put the second wing into position on the back of the bird, then take the needle back through the second wing hole and into the second wing. Make

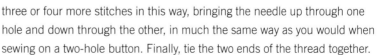

three or four more stitches in this way, bringing the needle up through one hole and down through the other, in much the same way as you would when sewing on a two-hole button. Finally, tie the two ends of the thread together.

8 Push the string or ribbon through the hanging hole at the top of the bird, using a twisting action. Make a loose knot halfway up the string and give the piece a tug down. Tie the loose ends together in an overhand knot.

Three LITTLE HOUSES

Whenever I am at the coast, I love to see the houses lined up on the harbor edge. This is what gave me the inspiration for this set of three houses. They sit perfectly on your mantelpiece and give a nice homely touch.

YOU WILL NEED:

Materials

Templates on page 140

Planed pine, approx. 40 x 3 x 1½–2 in. (1000 x 75 x 40–50 mm)

Square dowel/beading, approx. 10 x ⅜ x ⅜ in. (250 x 10 x 10 mm)

Water-based medium colored wood stain (optional)

Water-based paint in colors of your choice

Equipment

Tracing paper, pencil, and cardstock

Workbench

Clamps

Miter saw

Engineering square

Tenon saw

Hand plane (for general-purpose woodwork)

Dust mask

Safety goggles

Coarse and fine sandpaper

Glue gun and glue sticks

Masking tape

Medium flat, fine flat, and fine round paintbrushes

CUTTING LIST

Item	Number of pieces to cut	Dimensions (length)	Material
House 1	1	10⅝ in. (270 mm)	Planed pine
House 2	1	9¼ in. (235 mm)	Planed pine
House 3	1	8¼ in. (210 mm)	Planed pine

1 Securely clamp the miter saw to the work bench and use it to cut three pieces to the lengths given in the cutting list.

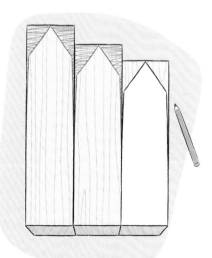

2 Following the instructions on pages 127 and 136, enlarge and trace the templates on page 140, then transfer them onto cardstock. Cut out the cardstock templates, and draw around them on the wood; it is useful to mark the waste wood that will be cut off.

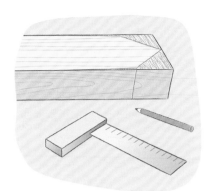

3 Use the engineering square to draw the roof lines on the sides of each piece of wood. This will give you a square cutting line.

4 Securely clamp the first piece of wood to the workbench. Using a tenon saw, cut out the roof shape (see page 120).

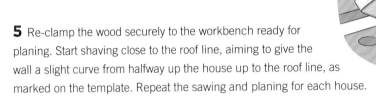

5 Re-clamp the wood securely to the workbench ready for planing. Start shaving close to the roof line, aiming to give the wall a slight curve from halfway up the house up to the roof line, as marked on the template. Repeat the sawing and planing for each house.

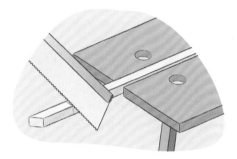

6 Using the chimney template on page 140, mark the roof angle on the length of square dowel/beading. Securely clamp the wood to the workbench and cut using the tenon saw. This will cut the chimney to the angle needed for it to fit on the roof, although you may need to sand it a little to get the angle just right. Mark the length of the chimney and use the engineering square to mark your lines for a straight cut. Repeat to cut three chimneys, each 1½ in. (40 mm) long.

7 Lightly sand the chimneys, taking care not to change the angle while sanding. Sand the houses, then rub the pieces with an old cloth to remove any dust (see page 131).

8 Place the first chimney on the roof and mark where it will sit. Apply a drop of glue to the chimney. Working quickly, carefully place the chimney in position and press down firmly. Hold in place until the glue has set. Repeat for the other two chimneys.

9 If you wish, apply wood stain to each house in turn, either using a brush or rubbing it on with an old cloth. Leave to dry completely. The wood stain will raise the wood fibers, so the houses will need a light sanding with fine sandpaper.

10 Using the templates on page 140, make a tracing-paper template of the painting lines for each house. Mark the painting lines for the roof and the front of each house. (You may want to use masking tape to mark these lines, to give a clean edge to the painting.) Paint the roof in your chosen color, using a medium flat paintbrush. Depending on the quality of the paint, you may need to apply two or three coats (see page 131). Then paint the front of the house.

11 Mark the position of the windows and the door. Paint them using a fine, flat paintbrush. Finally, use a very fine round brush to paint in the cross bars on the windows.

Matryoshka BOOKENDS

This pair of decorated bookends is a lovely project for a child's bedroom and will help to keep the bookshelves tidy. Like many of the projects in the book, you can substitute other motifs such as the bird or the heart on page 10, or change the colors to match the decor of the room.

YOU WILL NEED:

Materials

Template on page 136

Planed pine, approx. 31½ x 4½ x ¾ in. (800 x 110 x 20 mm), for the bookends

Planed pine, approx. 16 x 3 x ¼–½ in. (400 x 70 x 6–12 mm), for the dolls

Four no. 6 x 1¾-in. (45-mm) wood screws

White water-based paint for bookends

Water-based paints in your chosen colors for the dolls

Equipment

Clamps

Workbench

Miter saw

Pencil

Dust mask

Coarse, medium, and fine sandpaper

Engineering square

Safety goggles

Drill

⅜-in. (10-mm) Forstner bit

⅛-in. (3-mm) drill bit

Wood glue

Medium flat paint brush and various sizes for detail painting

Tracing paper

Coping saw

CUTTING LIST

Item	Number of pieces to cut	Dimensions (length)	Material
Bases	2	5½ x 4½ in. (140 x 110 mm)	Planed pine
Verticals	2	6¼ x 4½ in. (160 x 110 mm)	Planed pine

1 Securely clamp the miter saw to the workbench. Cut the four main pieces, following the cutting list; a miter saw will ensure that the cuts are square. To help you to identify the pieces, mark the vertical and base pieces with a pencil.

2 Place the vertical on the base to check that the edges are square and the vertical sits flat. If it does not, then try the other end or sand the face until it sits well. (The best way to sand the vertical is place a piece of coarse sandpaper flat on the workbench and rub the bottom of the vertical over it, keeping the vertical piece upright as you sand. Continue until the vertical rests flat.) Mark an "X" on the bottom face of the vertical, as you now know that this is a true square edge. Look over the base piece, decide which face has the fewest marks, and make a small pencil mark to make this face easily identifiable. This is now the top face.

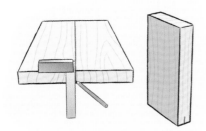

3 Measure and mark the center of the base piece across the width in two places, then place a ruler up to these marks to draw a line. Using an engineering square continue this line over the sides and along the underside of the piece.

4 Measure and mark the center of the upright side of the vertical piece.

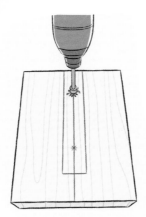

5 Place the vertical on the underside of the base, centered over the line drawn in step 3 with one end aligned with the edge of the base, and draw around it. Measure and mark two drill holes, 1 in. (25 mm) in from edges of the outline you have drawn. Using the ⅜-in. (10-mm) Forstner bit, drill holes on the marks until the cylindrical cutter is flush with the wood; the hole will be about ⁵⁄₁₆ in. (8 mm) deep—do not drill all the way through. This creates a rebate for the screw.

6 Clamp the vertical piece of the bookend into the workbench. Place the base on top of the vertical piece, with the drill holes facing upward. Look underneath to check that the marks you have made all line up. Using a ⅛-in. (3-mm) drill bit, drill through one of the Forstner holes on the base into the vertical piece, creating a pilot hole. Lightly screw the two pieces together, check that it is still lined up, and then drill the second pilot hole in the same way.

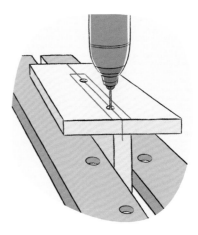

7 Unscrew the base, leaving the vertical in the workbench. Apply glue to the edge face of the vertical piece. Put the base back on the vertical and screw the pieces together tightly. Wipe away any glue that has seeped out. Repeat steps 2–7 to make the second bookend.

8 Paint the bookends with white water-based paint. Leave to dry completely, then lightly sand the edges to remove any raised grain. Apply the next coat of paint. Depending on the quality of the paint, you may need to apply two or three coats (see page 131).

9 Trace the Russian doll template on page 136, cut out, and check that it fits your piece of wood. Draw around the template onto the wood twice, making sure that the templates lie with the grain of the wood. Clamp the wood to the workbench, then cut both pieces using a coping saw. Sand the edges of the bookends and the edges of one face of each doll, then rub the pieces with an old cloth to remove any dust (see page 131).

10 Trace the painting lines on the template for the Russian doll onto one side of each doll-shaped piece of wood. Using a small round paintbrush, paint in the details in your chosen colors in the following order, allowing the paint to dry between each stage: center of main body, outer edges of main body, flesh tone of the face, hair, head scarf. As with the bookends, you may need to apply two or three coats of each color.

11 Change to a very fine round brush and paint the facial details, main flower color, flower details, and dots around the center of the main body (see page 132).

12 Put the two bookends together as though in use. When the dolls are completely dry, use wood glue to apply them to the front of the bookend verticals.

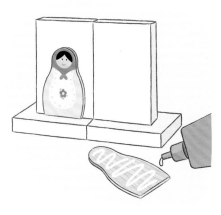

Candle BOX

This is a traditional country-style piece, although the simplicity of the design means that it will fit into many styles of décor. The box is designed to hang on the wall and looks lovely with candles in, but it could also be used for wooden spoons or pencils. This project is finished with a gothic arch—but be inspired and design your own simple shape for the top.

YOU WILL NEED:

Materials

Template on page 142
Planed pine, 36 x 3½ x ½ in. (900 x 90 x 15 mm)
Plywood, 5 x 5 x ⅜ in. (120 x 120 x 9 mm), for base
1¼-in. (30-mm) brads or panel pins
Water-based wood primer
Water-based satinwood paint

Equipment

Clamps
Workbench
Miter saw
Tracing paper, pencil, and cardstock
Coping saw
Dust mask
Coarse and fine sandpaper
Bradawl

Wood glue
Tack/pin hammer
Electric sander
Nail punch
Wood filler
Steel ruler
Hand or panel saw
Safety goggles
Drill and ⅜-in. (10-mm) Forstner bit
Paintbrushes

CUTTING LIST

Item	Number of pieces to cut	Dimensions (length)	Material
Front	1	5 x 3½ in. (130 x 90 mm)	Planed pine
Back	1	11½ x 3½ in. (290 x 90 mm)	Planed pine
Side panels	2	5 x 2¾ in. (130 x 70 mm)	Planed pine

1 Securely clamp the miter saw to the workbench. Use the miter saw, to cut the wood to the lengths specified in the cutting list. You should now have four pieces for the candle box. Label each piece for later identification.

2 Following the instructions on pages 127 and 136, enlarge and trace the template for the back panel on page 142, then transfer it onto cardstock and cut out. Draw around it on the wood and mark the hole for hanging.

3 Securely clamp the wood for the back panel to the workbench. Using a coping saw, cut out the gothic arch (see page 121); you may need to re-clamp the wood as you cut around it. Lightly sand all four panels to remove any break-out from the sawing process.

4 Place the back panel on the workbench, with one side panel in position along the edge. Draw a line along the inside edge of the side panel to show the area in which you will place the brads/panel pins. Repeat with the other side panel.

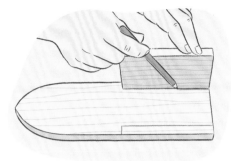

5 Place the front panel on the workbench. Repeat step 4 to mark the area where the brads/panel pins will go.

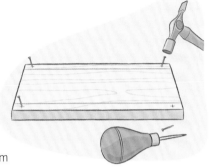

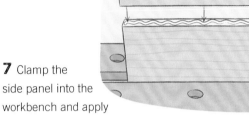

6 Measure approx. ½ in. (12 mm) in from one corner of the front panel, then make a mark level with this point halfway between the edge of the panel and the line drawn in step 5. Repeat at each corner. Use a bradawl to start a hole at each point, then tap in a brad/panel pin at an angle, until it is just protruding out through the wood underneath.

7 Clamp the side panel into the workbench and apply a line of glue to the surface that will butt up to the front panel. Place the front panel on the side panel and push together, making sure that the edges are flush.

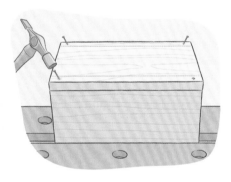

8 Tap the two panel pins all the way in to secure the front to the side, working slowly and carefully to avoid the pins changing angles and splitting the wood.

9 Now apply glue to the other side panel and butt the top panel against it. (You will not be able to clamp this side panel into the workbench.) Make sure that the edges are flush; if they are not, make sure the same end is flush as on the first side panel. Tap in the two brad/panel pins carefully and evenly. If one of the brad/panel pins comes through the wood, use pliers to remove the pin and start with a new one. Wipe off any excess glue and leave to dry completely.

10 Decide which end will be the base of the box: this should be the end where the 3 panels joined are the flattest. Hold the box against the back panel to check that the box will sit flat and square. You may want to sand the top edges of the box at this stage to get an even, flat surface.

11 Repeat steps 6–9 to attach the back panel to the side panels; for the two top pins, you will need to measure ½ in. (12 mm) down from the line marking the top edge of the side panel.

12 Use a nail punch to knock the heads of the brads/panel pins just beneath the wood. Following the manufacturer's instructions, apply wood filler to the panel pin holes and leave to set.

13 Place the candle box on the plywood for the base, making sure that the back edge is flush with the straight edge of the plywood. Draw around the base of the box. To mark out the lines for the overhang, remove the box and draw another set of lines ¼ in. (6 mm) outside of the lines you have just drawn.

14 Securely clamp the plywood to the bench and cut along the waste side of the line, using a hand or panel saw (see page 121).

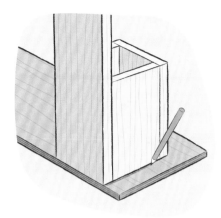

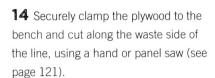

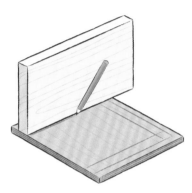

15 Sand the edges of the base panel, using coarse sandpaper or an electric sander. Take care to avoid splinters. Sand the candle box all over apart from the base edge. (You do not want to change the profile of this edge, as you have already checked that it sits flat on the base.) Sand until you have the shape and finish you want.

16 Place the candle box on the reverse of the base, with the back edge flush with the edge of the plywood and the same amount overhanging on the other three sides. Draw around the box. Place an off-cut of wood on the inside of your drawn lines and draw another line; this will indicate the thickness of the wood and show you the area in which you will attach the brads/panel pins.

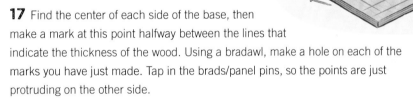

17 Find the center of each side of the base, then make a mark at this point halfway between the lines that indicate the thickness of the wood. Using a bradawl, make a hole on each of the marks you have just made. Tap in the brads/panel pins, so the points are just protruding on the other side.

18 Place the box upside down in the workbench and apply a wiggly line of glue. Place the base in position, taking care to make the overhang equal. You should still be able to see a little of your pencil lines which will help you to line it up. Push the base panel down firmly. Tap in the brad/panel pin on the back edge, then the front pin, and finally the side pins. Use the nail punch to tap the pin heads in further. Check the box over and sand any remaining areas that need it.

19 Using a ⅜-in. (10-mm) Forstner bit, drill the hole for hanging (see page 133).

20 Apply wood primer to the candle box if necessary. Paint the candle box in your chosen color (see page 131); depending on the quality of the paint, you may need to apply two or three coats.

Hanging MOON

The first time I made this lovely moon was for a friend when I was living in Greece—so for me it is something that brings back lots of lovely memories. I love the simplicity of this moon shape, which is why I have kept the paint technique to a minimum and just finished it with a couple of coats of wax, giving it a nice, soft sheen. The added bead makes it perfect for hanging in the window.

YOU WILL NEED:

Materials

Template on page 139

Planed pine, 12 x 8 x ½–¾ in. (300 x 200 x 15–20 mm)

Water-based paint in color of your choice

Small screw eye

4 in. (10 cm) thin wire

Bead

String or ribbon to hang

Equipment

Clamps

Workbench

Tracing paper, pencil, and cardstock

Coping saw

Dust mask

Safety goggles

Drill and ⁹⁄₆₄-in. (3.5-mm) bit

Surform block plane or rasp

Coarse and fine sandpaper

Bradawl

Wire cutters and pliers

1 Following the instructions on pages 127 and 136, enlarge and trace the moon template on page 139, then transfer onto cardstock and cut out. Place the template on the wood and draw around it, taking the grain of the wood into account.

2 Using a coping saw and referring to the diagram for the order of cutting, cut out the moon (see page 121); you may need to re-clamp the piece as you cut around it.

3 Using the template, mark where the hanging hole is to be drilled. Drill the hole using a ⁹⁄₆₄-in. (3.5-mm) bit.

4 Use the surform plane or rasp to round the outside edge of the moon (see page 123), using light strokes to create a smooth edge.

5 Sand the moon shape, then rub with an old cloth to remove any dust (see page 131). Paint the moon in your chosen color. Depending on the quality of the paint, you may need to apply two or three coats (see page 131).

6 Use the template to mark the position of the screw eye that hangs from the inside of the forehead. Use the bradawl to start the hole and then twist the screw eye into position. You may need to use pliers to help twist it in further.

7 Thread the bead on to the small length of wire, then loop the wire through the screw eye and twist the ends together to secure. Trim the wire.

8 Push the string or ribbon through the hanging hole at the top of the moon, using a twisting action. Make a loose knot halfway up the string and give the piece a tug down. Tie the loose ends together in an overhand knot and trim the ends to neaten.

Coat HOOKS

This project is designed to give you the confidence to cut and shape a panel of wood, so whenever you see some hooks that you really like, you will know exactly what to do with them. Apart from cutting the wood, the only rules are to make sure the spacing for the hooks looks good to the eye, the hooks are attached properly, and the finished project is securely mounted to the wall. I chose these hand-forged wrought-iron hooks—they go well with the simplicity of the piece and give it a lovely rustic look.

YOU WILL NEED:

Materials

Template on page 141

Planed pine, 24 x 7¾ x ¾ in. (610 x 195 x 20 mm), for the back panel

Planed pine, 15 x 4 x ¼–⁵⁄₁₆ in. (380 x 100 x 6–8 mm), for the hearts

Three decorative hooks approx. 3½ in. (90 mm) long with screws

Water-based paint

Water-based matt acrylic varnish (optional)

Decorative paper

PVA glue

Wood glue

Equipment

Tri-square

Retractable tape measure

Pencil

Clamps

Workbench

Hand or panel saw

Tracing paper, pencil, and cardstock

Dust mask

Safety goggles

Drill and ¼-in. (6-mm) bit

Countersink bit

Jigsaw

Coping saw

Electric sander or coarse and fine sandpaper

Bradawl

Small slotted (flat-headed) screwdriver

Paintbrush

1 Using the tri-square, check that one end of the back panel is square. If it is not, then use the tri-square to draw a square, straight line and saw along this line using the hand or panel saw. From your square edge, measure and mark 20 in. (51 mm) along the length of the back panel and use the tri-square to draw a square, straight line. Clamp the wood securely to the workbench and cut to length using a hand or panel saw.

2 Following the instructions on pages 127 and 136, enlarge and trace the template on page 141, then transfer onto cardstock and cut out. Place the template in one of the top corners of the back panel and draw around it. Move to the other top corner and again draw around the template again; this creates the curves ready for cutting with the jigsaw.

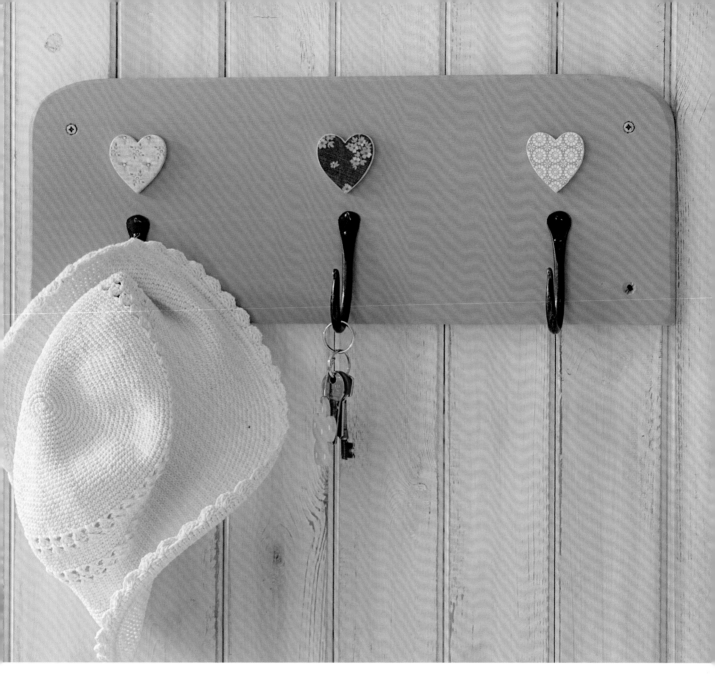

3 Following the diagram, mark the position of the four screw holes that will be used to hang the coat hook to the wall. Drill the screw holes using the ¼-in. (6-mm) bit. Countersink the holes.

4 Securely clamp the back panel to the workbench. Cut out the two curves, using a jigsaw (see page 121). You will need to re-clamp often to maneuver the jigsaw around the cutting line and the clamps.

5 Transfer the hearts from the template in step 2 onto cardstock and cut out. Draw around the heart template three times on the wood, using the back panel template as a position guide. Securely clamp the wood to the workbench. Use a coping saw to cut out each heart. (For this size, it is too dangerous to use the electric jigsaw.)

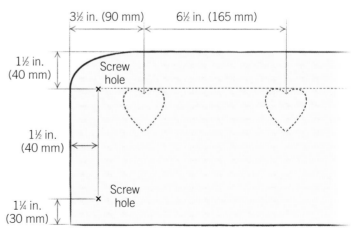

3½ in. (90 mm)   6½ in. (165 mm)

1½ in. (40 mm)   Screw hole

1½ in. (40 mm)

1¼ in. (30 mm)   Screw hole

6 Sand the back panel and the hearts until you have the finish and shape you require (see page 123). You may prefer to use an electric sander on the back panel, as this will make lighter work if you are rounding off the edges of the panel. Rub the pieces over with an old cloth to remove any dust.

7 Draw a line across the back panel between the two top screw holes. Referring to the diagram for step 3, mark the points at which the dip in the center of the hearts will align. Place the three hearts in position. Place the two end hooks in position first, each below a heart. The height at which you place the hooks will depend on the type you buy, so move the hook higher or lower on the back panel until you are happy with its position. Use a bradawl to mark through the screw holes in the hooks onto the back panel. (The position of the holes will vary for different styles of hook.)

8 Choose a suitable drill bit for the size of screws you are using (see page 124) and drill a pilot hole for each screw at the points you have just marked with the bradawl. Lightly screw the two end hooks in position. Place a tape measure or ruler across the top of these hooks to find the height of the center hook. Use the bradawl to mark the screw holes, drill the pilot holes, and lightly screw into place. Check you are happy with the position of the hooks and hearts, then set them to one side in preparation for painting. You may need to sand around the screw holes to remove any break-out from drilling.

9 Paint the back panel in your chosen color. Depending on the quality of the paint, you may need to apply two or three coats (see page 131). To seal and protect the paint, apply a water-based varnish over the paint (see page 131).

10 I painted the hearts in the same color as the back panel; you only need to paint the sides of each heart. Leave the paint to dry, then apply the decorative paper to each heart (see page 133).

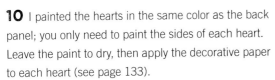

11 Tightly screw the hooks back into place, remembering to realign the screw holes for each hook.

12 The marks for placing the hearts have been painted over. To avoid making any more pencil lines, place a retractable tape measure across the two upper screw holes: this gives you the height again for the hearts. Place each heart in line with the tops of the hooks. Apply a small amount of glue to the backs of the hearts and push back down into position. Remove any excess glue and leave to dry completely.

Boot HOLDER

This is a fun, practical project that keeps your boots tidy and dry. Just imagine a whole row lined up by the back door for those rainy days. There is a good range of colors for exterior paint or wood stain on the market, so there's no excuse not to be bright and bold. The construction is simple and this is a good project to do before stepping up to the bigger ones, such as the tool box on page 48.

YOU WILL NEED:

Materials

These dimensions are for a set of child-sized boots; for an adult, just cut the dowel to a longer length. Use off-cuts from other projects to make it.

Planed pine, approx. 16 x 1¾ x ½–⅝ in. (400 x 45 x 15 mm)

Planed pine, approx. 10 x 2¾ x ¾ in. (250 x 70 x 20 mm)

25-in. (620-mm) length of pine dowel, 1 in. (25 mm) in diameter

Four no. 6 x 1-in. (25-mm) wood screws
Two no. 6 x 1½-in. (40-mm) wood screws
Wood stain or water-based exterior paint in two colors

Equipment

Clamps
Miter saw
Workbench
Pencil and steel ruler
Dust mask
Safety goggles

Drill and ⅛-in. (3-mm) bit
1-in. (25-mm) Forstner bit
Countersinking bit/tool
Engineering square
Electric sander or coarse and fine sandpaper
Screwdriver
Wood glue
Paintbrushes

1 Securely clamp the miter saw to the workbench and use it to cut all the pieces for the boot holder. From 1¾-in.- (45-mm-) wide pine cut two 7½-in. (190-mm) lengths for the base supports. From 2¾-in.- (70-mm-) wide pine, cut one 7-in. 180-mm) length for the base panel. Cut two 12-in. (305-mm) lengths of dowel for the pegs. Label each piece for later identification.

2 Following the diagram, mark the position of the holes that are to be drilled through the base panel.

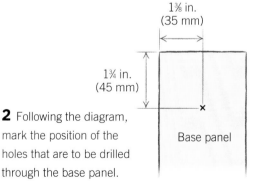

1⅜ in. (35 mm)

1¾ in. (45 mm)

Base panel

3 Place the base panel on a scrap piece of wood and securely clamp to the workbench. Drill the two holes with a 1-in. (25-mm) Forstner bit, keeping the drill as vertical as possible.

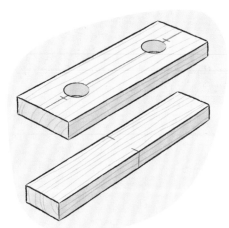

4 Using a steel ruler and pencil, draw a line down the center of the base panel from one short end to the other. At each end of the base panel, make a mark 1 in. (25 mm) in from the edge on the line you have just drawn. Now mark the halfway point along each long side of the two base supports.

5 Mark the holes for drilling on the base supports from the diagram.

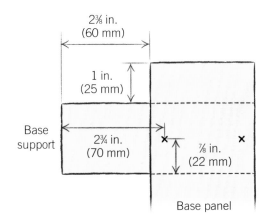

2⅜ in. (60 mm)

1 in. (25 mm)

Base support

2¾ in. (70 mm)

⅞ in. (22 mm)

Base panel

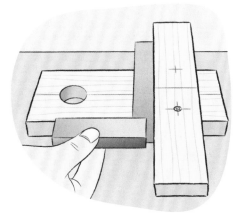

6 Place the base panel on the workbench. Place one of the base supports on top, aligning the pencil lines on both pieces. Using a ⅛-in. (3-mm) bit, drill a hole, then countersink this hole. Lightly screw together using a 1-in. (25-mm) screw, then check that the base support is square with the base panel using an engineering square. Now drill the other hole, countersink it, and screw the panels together tightly. Repeat step 5 for the other base support.

7 Using a ⅛-in. (3-mm) bit, drill a central hole between each rebate and through each base support; this is for the dowel pegs. Remove any break-out from the drilling so that the dowel pegs will sit flush on the base supports. Countersink the holes on the underside of the base supports.

8 Using either an electric sander or coarse and fine sandpaper, sand all the pieces to remove any break-out from the sawing or until you have the finish you require. Sand one end of the dowel pegs. You may wish to sand these to a rounded finish. Rub over with an old cloth to remove any dust (see page 131).

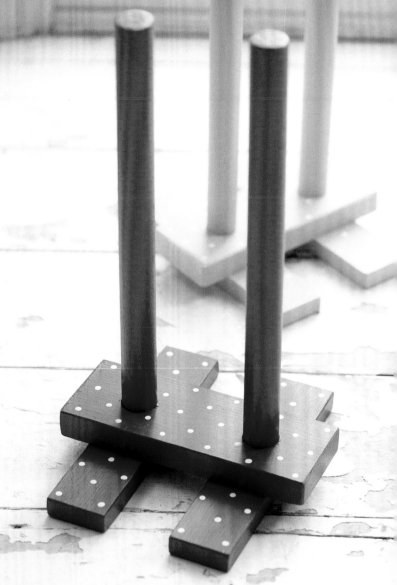

9 Apply a small amount of glue into the rebate for the dowel peg. Push the dowel peg into position with a twisting action. Twist and manipulate the dowel peg so that it sits vertically. Place a 1½-in. (45-mm) screw in the hole of the base support that you made in step 6 and screw the dowel peg and the base together tightly. Repeat for the other dowel peg.

10 Paint with a water-based outdoor wood stain in your chosen color. Depending on the quality of the exterior paint or wood stain, you may need two or more coats (see page 131). When the final base coat was dry, I added tiny polka dots in white paint (see page 132), but you could leave the boot pegs all in one color if you prefer.

Shelf

This is a project that can be made for any room around the house, and you can easily make it longer or shorter, depending on where it's going. It's a very satisfying feeling to make your own shelf and know that you have not relied on others to make or hang it for you. The shelf can be decorated in whatever color you like; I love a touch of vintage style, so I also added lace around the edge.

YOU WILL NEED:

Materials

Template on page 137

Planed pine approx, 19 x 6 x ¾ in. (480 x 150 x 20 mm) for shelf

Planed pine, 20 x 6 x ¾ in. (500 x 150 x 20 mm) for brackets

Four No. 6 x 1½-in. (40-mm) wood screws

Wood glue

Water-based paint in two colors of your choice

Water-based matt varnish

Lace trim to fit the sides and front edge of the shelf (optional)

Equipment

Tracing paper, pencil, and cardstock

Tri-square

Workbench

Clamps

Jigsaw/coping saw

Miter saw

Dust mask

Safety goggles

Electric sander (optional)

Coarse and fine sandpaper

Tape measure

Drill and ⅛-in. (3-mm) drill bit

Countersink bit/tool

Screwdriver

Paintbrushes

Latex glue

1 Following the instructions on page 127, trace the template for the brackets on page 137, transfer onto cardstock, and cut out. Place the back edge of the bracket template on the flat edge of the wood, then use the tri-square to ensure that the right angle of the bracket is square. Draw around the template twice: it needs to be precise, otherwise the shelf will not sit flat.

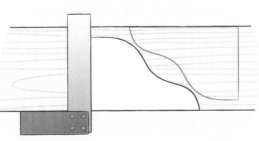

WHEN PLACING YOUR TEMPLATES, TRY TO AVOID KNOTS AND ANY DEFECTS IN THE WOOD, AS THIS COULD AFFECT YOUR FINAL FINISH.

2 If you are using a jigsaw to cut the brackets, open up the workbench as much as possible and clamp the wood so that the curved cutting line on the bracket is placed in the center of your workbench. Cut the curve of the bracket, then use the miter saw to cut along the right angle of that bracket. If you are using a coping saw to cut the curve, cut the right angle first using the miter saw, then cut the curved edge of the bracket with the coping saw. Repeat the cutting process for the other bracket.

3 If you are happy with the length of the shelf from the materials list, then go straight to the next step; otherwise use the miter saw to cut your shelf to the length you want.

4 Sand away any break-out from the sawing process.

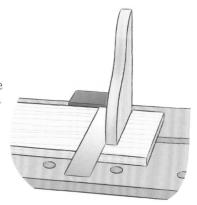

5 Place the shelf panel on the workbench. Measure and mark 2½ in. (65 mm) in from each end. Place the outer edge of a bracket up to one of these marks, then place the tri-square on the inside edge of the bracket to ensure it is sitting nice and square on the shelf panel. Draw around the base of the bracket; this is the area in which you will drill the screw holes. Repeat for the other bracket.

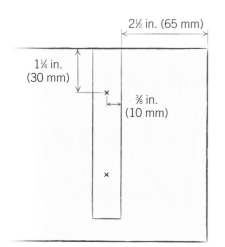

2½ in. (65 mm)

1¼ in. (30 mm)

⅜ in. (10 mm)

6 Referring to the diagram (see left), mark the position of the screw holes.

7 Using a ⅛-in. (3-mm) bit, drill all the way through the wood at all four marked points. On the other face of the shelf panel, countersink the holes (see page 128). Place a screw in each hole and screw them in until the points protrude through the wood the other side.

8 Put the shelf panel down on the workbench on its back edge. Locate the bracket to the marked area you made earlier and push the bracket up hard against the screw points; the screws should leave a mark in the top edge of the bracket. Remove the bracket and use a bradawl to enlarge the marked holes. Locate the bracket back on the screw points and screw together tightly. Repeat for the other bracket.

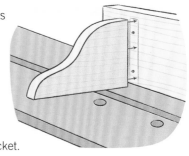

9 Using either an electric sander or sandpaper, sand the shelf down until you have the shape and finish you require.

10 Paint the shelf in your chosen color and finish; I used a rustic paint finish (see page 132); depending on the quality of the paint, you may need to apply more than one coat. Coat the shelf in a water-based matt varnish to seal the paint and leave to dry completely.

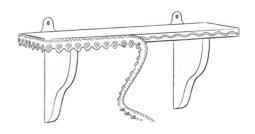

11 Attach the shelf to the wall (see pages 133–135); I suggest using glass/mirror plates.

12 If you wish, glue a length of vintage lace trim around the shelf edge.

Box FRAME

This is an easy but very effective technique to make a box frame. It can be used to display pretty paper or fabric, or one of your favorite pieces of artwork that you or your children have created. The back panel can easily be removed, allowing you to change the contents.

YOU WILL NEED:

Materials

Template on page 140

Planed pine floorboard, 40 x 4⅜ in. (1000 x 110 mm)

Square dowel/beading, 49 x ¾ x ¾ in. (1250 x 20 x 20 mm)

Two pieces plywood, each 13 x 13 x ³⁄₁₆–⅜-in. (330 x 330 x 5–9 mm)

⅝-in. (15-mm) brads or panel pins

1¼-in. (30-mm) brads or panel pins

Four No. 6 x ¾-in. (20-mm) wood screws

Water-based paint in your chosen color

Equipment

Workbench

Clamps

Miter saw

Hand plane

Tack/pin hammer

Drill

⅛- and ⅜-in. (3- and 10-mm) bits

Jigsaw

Dust mask

Safety goggles

Sandpaper or electric sander

Flat-head screwdriver

Countersink bit

Nail punch

Tri-square

Tape measure

Tracing paper, pencil, and cardstock

Steel ruler

Wood glue

Paintbrush

1 Securely clamp the miter saw to the workbench and cut three 12⅝-in. (320-mm) lengths of floorboard; the miter saw will ensure that the cuts are square.

2 Place the three floorboard panels together and number them 1, 2, and 3, so that you will know which order they go in. You will need to remove the tongue from the outside edge of panel 1 and the groove from the outside edge of panel 3. Securely clamp panel 1 into the workbench, with the tongue facing upward. Use the hand plane to remove the tongue from what will be the outside edge.

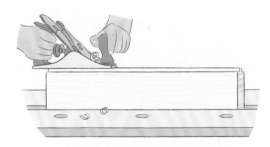

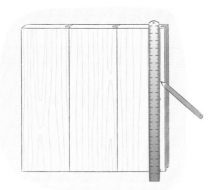

3 Now put the three panels together again in the correct order. Measure across the top from the panel you have just planed and make a pencil mark at 12⅝ in. (320 mm); repeat across the bottom and middle of the panels. Using the steel ruler, draw a line across to join the marks up.

4 Now place panel 3 in the workbench and plane away the groove from what will be the outside edge until you reach the line you have just drawn. When assembled, the three panels should be square and measure 12⅝ in. (320 mm) in each direction.

5 Apply glue to the tongue and the groove of each panel. Push the panels together to make one big panel and remove any excess glue. Place the panel on a flat surface so that it does not twist as it dries. Leave to dry completely. Choose the best face and mark it; this is the face you will see on the front of the frame.

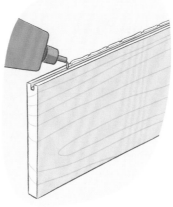

6 Use ⅝-in. (15-mm) brad or panel pins to attach one of the plywood boards to the back of the panel; this will strengthen the panel, ready for cutting with the jigsaw later. Place a brad or panel pin in each corner of the plywood approx. 1½ in. (38 mm) in from the edge and tap it in, making sure that the heads are flush with the wood.

7 Following the instructions on pages 127 and 136, enlarge and trace the heart template on page 140, then transfer onto cardstock and cut out. Measure across the best face of the panel, mark the center in two places, then use the steel ruler to join the marks up and draw a line down the center. Place the heart so that the point and the dip of the heart are on the line, with the dip of the heart 3½ in. (90 mm) from the top of the panel. Draw around the template onto the panel.

8 Using a ⅜-in. (10-mm) bit, drill a hole approx. ½ in. (12 mm) down from the dip of the heart. Securely clamp the frame panel to the workbench. Place the jigsaw blade in the drill hole and cut out the heart shape (see page 121).

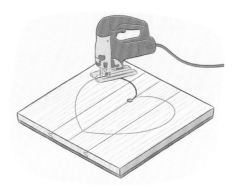

9 Using a flat-headed screwdriver, lever off the plywood from the back of the frame panel. Remove the panel pins from the plywood for your safety. (Keep this off-cut to use in another project.)

10 You are now ready to attach the square dowel/beading to the back of the panel to form a square frame. Cut two 12⅝-in. (320-mm) lengths, using the miter saw. Tap in one 1¼-in. (30-mm) brad or panel pin approx. 2 in. (50 mm) from each end at an angle of about 45°. The point of the brad or panel pin needs to just show through the wood.

11 Apply a wiggly line of glue to one length of square dowel/beading and place it on one side of the frame, making sure it is flush with the edges. Using the tack/pin hammer, tap the brads or panel pins into the frame. If necessary, use the nail punch to finish. Attach the second length of square dowel/beading to the other side of the frame in the same way. Remove any excess glue.

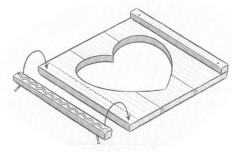

12 Measure the gap between the two pieces of square dowel/beading that you have attached to the frame panel. Mark these measurements on the remaining length of square dowel/beading and cut to length using the miter saw. Attach them to the top and bottom of the frame panel in the same way as the first two lengths. Leave until completely dry.

13 Place the remaining piece of ply on the back of the frame so that there is a small, even overhang all around. Find the center of each side on the ply and mark it approx. ⅜ in. (10 mm) in from the edge. Using a ⅛-in. (3-mm) bit, drill a hole at the first marked point, taking care not to drill all the way through the picture frame. Countersink the hole, insert a ¾-in. (20-mm) screw, and tighten. Repeat for other three screws.

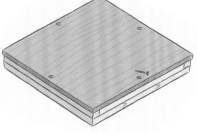

14 Plane and sand the ply until it is flush with the frame. Sand the whole picture frame until you have the shape and finish you require (see page 131).

15 Paint the frame in your chosen color; depending on the quality of the paint, you may need to apply two or three coats (see page 131).

CHAPTER 2

KITCHEN AND BATHROOM

The projects in this chapter are slightly more challenging, but the techniques required are simple and use basic hand tools. As you repeat certain skills, you'll soon improve and find you are able to make very impressive items, such as the mug cupboard (page 70), creating a home that looks truly handmade!

Three LITTLE FISHES

Many bathrooms have a nautical theme, so these charming little fish will fit right in. You can display them next to your flotilla of boats (see page 52). Choose different thicknesses of wood to give each fish its own individual character. This is the perfect project for using off-cuts left over from other projects. The fish in the photograph have been rounded, but you could leave them with a flat face and use the découpage technique (see page 133) to apply nautical paper.

YOU WILL NEED:

Materials

Templates on page 140

Three pieces planed pine, each 10 x 3 x ⅜–¾in. (250 x 80 x 10–18mm)

Water-based paint in three coordinated colors

Rustic garden string, 12 in. (300 mm), for each fish

Equipment

Tracing paper, pencil, and cardstock

Workbench

Clamps

Coping saw

Dust mask

Safety goggles

Drill and ⁹⁄₆₄-in. (3.5-mm) drill bit

Round surform file or rasp

Coarse and fine sandpaper

Paintbrushes

Wooden toothpick

1 Following the instructions on pages 127 and 136, enlarge and trace the fish templates on page 140, then transfer onto cardstock. Cut out the templates and draw around them on the wood, keeping the grain of the wood running along the length of the fish. Mark where hanging holes are to be drilled.

2 Securely clamp the wood to the workbench. Cut out the shapes using a coping saw. (You may need to re-clamp the piece as you work around the line.) Drill the hanging holes using a ⁹⁄₆₄-in. (3.5-mm) bit (see page 124).

3 Working with the grain, use the surform file or rasp to shape your fish (see page 123). You can either place the fish on the edge of the workbench and slide the file over to shape it or work with both the file and the fish in your hands.

4 Sand the fish then, rub them with an old cloth to remove any dust (see page 131). Paint the fish with your chosen colors. Depending on the quality of the paint, you may need to apply two or three coats (see page 131).

5 Check the hanging holes: if they are blocked with paint, clear them out with a wooden toothpick. Cut three lengths of string and thread each string through the hanging hole from front to back. Tie a knot at the end of each string to form the "eye" of the fish, then cut off any excess string underneath the knot. Gather all the strings together and adjust the length, so that each fish hangs at a different height. Now tie the strings together in an overhand knot halfway down to create a hanging loop.

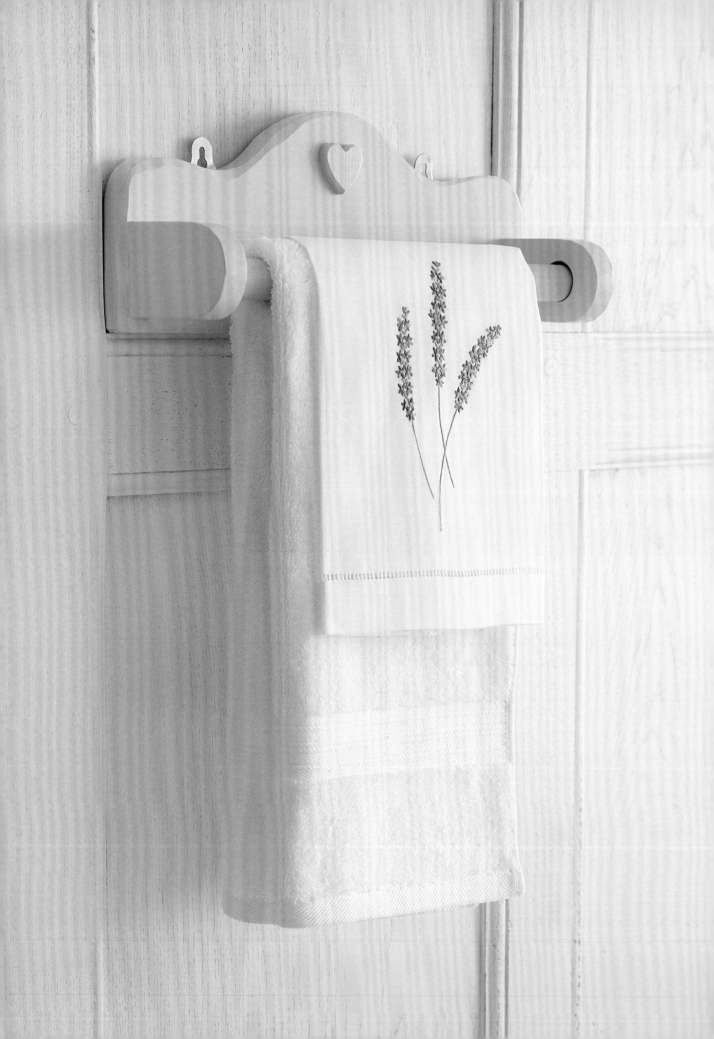

Towel RAIL

This project provides an introduction to more complicated woodworking techniques. Don't be put off by the dowel joint, as it is a great way to make a solid, strong joint for all types of projects. The size and color of the towel rail can be adapted to suit your bathroom and will give you the perfect excuse to go out and buy more pretty towels!

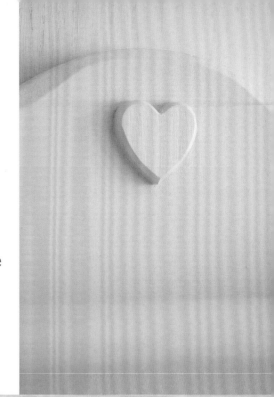

YOU WILL NEED:

Materials

Templates on page 139

Planed pine, 27½ x 6 x ¾ in. (700 x 150 x 20 mm) for the back and side panels

19-in. (480-mm) length of dowel, 1 in. (25 mm) in diameter, for the rail

Planed pine, 12 x 2¾ x ⅜ in. (300 x 7 x 6–10 mm), for the heart

Four ¼-in. (6-mm) fluted dowels

Two no. 6 x 1½-in. (45-mm) wood screws

Wood primer, if required

Quick-drying water-based satinwood or eggshell paint

Equipment

Tracing paper, pencil, and cardstock

Clamps

Workbench

Miter saw

Jigsaw with scroll-saw blade

Coping saw (optional)

Bradawl

Masking tape

Dust mask

Safety goggles

Drill and ⅛-in. (3-mm) drill bit

¼-in. (6-mm) dowel center-point marker kit

1-in. (25-mm) Forstner bit

Countersink bit

Coarse and fine sandpaper

Wood glue

Engineering square

Tri-square

Mallet

Paintbrushes

1 Following the instructions on pages 127 and 136, enlarge and trace the templates on page 139, then transfer onto cardstock and cut out. Place the back panel template on the length of pine and draw around it, avoiding any knots and defects that could affect the final finish. Use a tri-square to draw a line across the pine, place the base of the side panel template against this line, and draw around it twice.

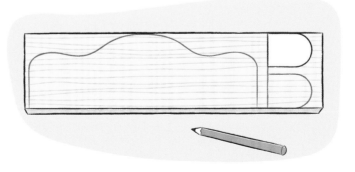

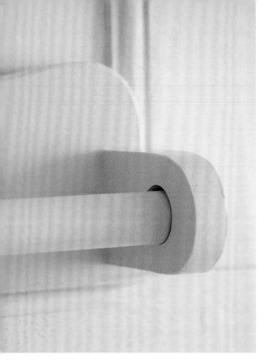

2 Securely clamp the pine to the workbench. Using an electric jigsaw (see page 121 for instructions and safety recommendations), cut out the back panel, repositioning the clamps as needed.

3 Securely clamp the miter saw to the workbench and saw along the straight line that you drew with the tri-square; this will be the straight edge that will attach to the back panel. Once this straight line is cut, clamp the pine to the workbench again and cut around the curve of the side panels with the jigsaw (see page 121). (You can use a coping saw if you prefer.)

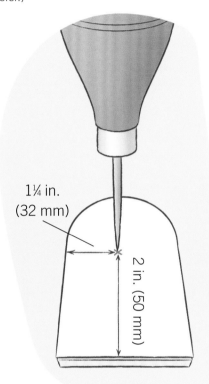

1¼ in. (32 mm)

2 in. (50 mm)

4 Place the template back on the cut-out side panel. Using a bradawl, mark where the rebate hole for the dowel rail is going to go. Using the 1-in. (25-mm) Forstner bit, drill a hole at each marked point until the cylindrical cutter is flush with the wood; the hole will be about ⅜ in. (10 mm) deep— do not drill all the way through. Repeat for the second side panel.

5 Now mark where the two side panels go. Choose the best face of the back panel. On the two bottom corners of the back panel, make a mark ⅜ in. (10 mm) in from the side and ⅜ in. (10 mm) up from the bottom. Put the side panels up against these marks and use the engineering square to make sure they are square to the back panel. Draw around the base of them, before putting them to one side. Make corresponding marks for the two joints, making sure the rebate hole for the dowel rail is facing inward.

6 Place the template on the back panel. Using a bradawl, mark through the template where the holes for the dowel joints and the screw support holes will be drilled.

7 Using the ⅛-in. (3-mm) drill bit, drill the screw support holes all the way through the back panel. Turn the back panel over. Where the holes have come through, countersink the holes (see page 128) ready for the screws.

8 You will now be using the dowel center-point marker kit (see page 124). The back panel will be panel 1; each side panel is panel 2. Follow steps 2–6 of the dowel instructions for Dowel Joints on pages 128–9.

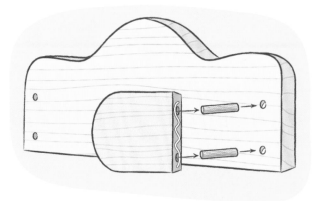

9 Place a small amount of glue in the dowel holes on one side of the back panel, and a wiggly line of glue along the surface of the corresponding side panel. Insert a fluted dowel into each hole and, using a mallet, tap the two panels together (see step 7 of Dowel Joints on page 129).

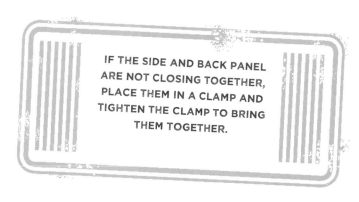

IF THE SIDE AND BACK PANEL ARE NOT CLOSING TOGETHER, PLACE THEM IN A CLAMP AND TIGHTEN THE CLAMP TO BRING THEM TOGETHER.

10 Working quickly, place a screw in the two pre-drilled holes of the back panel and screw in the side panel.

11 You are now ready to cut the dowel rail. Provided you have followed all the measurements given for this project, the space between the side panels will be 15⅛ in. (385 mm). Cut the dowel rail to 16 in. (405 mm), using a miter saw.

12 Place the dowel rail in the rebate of the attached side panel and then into the rebate of the other side panel. Attach the second side panel to the back panel in the same way as in step 10.

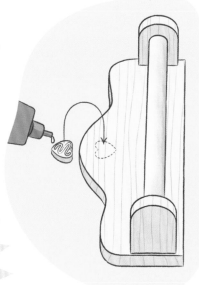

IN STEP 11, IF THE SPACE BETWEEN THE SIDE PANELS IS MORE THAN 15⅛ IN. (385 MM), YOU WILL NEED TO ADD THE EXTRA TO THE DOWEL RAIL MEASUREMENT OF 16 IN. (405 MM); IF IT IS LESS, SUBTRACT IT.

13 Trace the heart template on page 139, cut out, and draw around it on the wood, taking the grain of the wood into account. Securely clamp the wood to the workbench, then cut it out using a coping saw. (For this size of decoration, it is too dangerous to use the electric jigsaw.) Glue the heart in position, using the back panel template as a guide. Leave to dry.

14 Sand the towel rail, then rub the piece with an old cloth to remove any dust (see page 131).

15 Now you are ready for painting. Apply a wood primer (if needed), then sand down to remove any risen wood fiber. Apply your chosen paint, leaving to dry between coats. Depending on the quality of the paint, you may need to apply two or three coats (see page 131). Leave to dry before attaching the towel rail to the wall (see page 135).

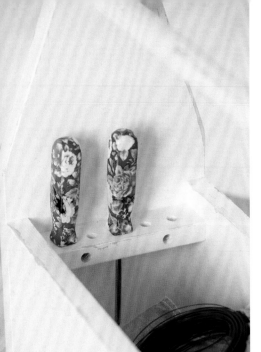

Tool BOX

This box can be adapted for so many things. Make one for yourself to store your tools and soon everyone will want one: it's just the right size for knitting projects, magazines, and all sorts of bits and pieces. It has been painted with a rustic finish so that it already looks well used and any more bumps and marks will enhance it further.

YOU WILL NEED:

Materials

Two planks of planed pine, approx. 35½ x 7⅝ x ¾ in. (900 x 195 x 20 mm)

20-in. (500-mm) length of round dowel, 1in (25mm) in diameter

Plywood, 20 x 9 x 3⁄16 in. (500 x 230 x 4 mm), for the base

Eight no. 6 x 1¾-in. (45-mm) wood screws

Two no. 6 x 1½-in. (40-mm) wood screws

1-in. (25-mm) panel pins

Dark brown and white water-based paint

Water-based clear matt varnish

Equipment

Pencil and metal ruler

Workbench

Clamps

Hand saw

Masking tape

Dust mask

Safety goggles

Drill

1- and ⅜-in. (25- and 10-mm) Forstner bits

⅛-in. (3-mm) drill bit

Coarse and fine sandpaper

Engineering square

Miter saw

Wood glue

Bradawl

Tack/pin hammer

Medium paintbrush

Engineering square

Latex-based adhesive

1 Securely clamp the wood to the workbench. Cut the wood into four 15-in. (380-mm) lengths for the end and side panels of the toolbox. Label each piece for later identification.

2 Now cut down the width of the side panels: measure 6 in. (150 mm) across the width of the side panel, make three marks along the length at the point, and draw a line along. Securely clamp the side panel to the workbench and use the hand saw to saw along the line (see page 121). Repeat for the other side panel. Keep one off-cut, as this will be used for the tool rest inside the box.

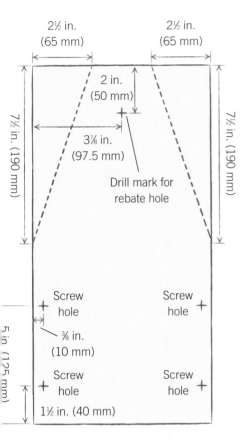

2½ in. (65 mm) 2½ in. (65 mm)

2 in. (50 mm)

7½ in. (190 mm)

3⅞ in. (97.5 mm)

Drill mark for rebate hole

7½ in. (190 mm)

Screw hole Screw hole

⅜ in. (10 mm)

5 in. (125 mm)

Screw hole Screw hole

1½ in. (40 mm)

3 To shape the tops of the end panels, make pencil marks 2½ in. (65 mm) in from each side of the top edge and 7½ in. (190 mm) down on the sides. Draw a line to join up the marks (shown as a dotted line in the diagram). Repeat on the other end panel. Decide which face of the two end panels is going to be the inside of the tool box and mark the position of the rebate hole for the dowel handle on this face. Turn the panels over and mark the position of the screw holes on the outside of the end panels. It is important that these are copied accurately.

4 Securely clamp the end panel to the workbench. Cut along the diagonal lines, using a hand saw; always cut on the waste side of the line. Repeat for the other end panel.

5 Apply a masking-tape marker to the 1-in. (25-mm) Forstner bit, ⁹⁄₁₆ in. (14 mm) from the point. Drill the rebate hole, taking care not to drill all the way through the wood. Repeat for the other end panel.

6 Using a ⅛-in. (3-mm) bit, drill the screw holes that you marked out on the end panels all the way through, drilling from the outside of the end panels. Change to a ⅜-in. (10-mm) Forstner bit and drill into the same holes to form rebates ⅛ in. (3 mm) deep; this is an alternative to using a countersink bit. Lightly sand away any break-out from the drilling, so that the inside of the side panel will sit tight against the end panel.

7 Now do a dry run before the final gluing. Place a 1¾-in. (45-mm) wood screw in each rebated hole in turn and screw until the screw tip is just showing though the other side; because you are screwing into end grain, it is not necessary to drill a pilot hole into the side panels. Do this for both end panels.

8 Place the end panel and one side panel together and push them together; the screw will push into the end grain of the side panel. Lightly screw the two panels together. Repeat with the other side panel, so that both side panels are attached to one end panel. Repeat for the other end panel. Use the engineering square to check that all pieces fit and are square. Label each joint on both panels, so that you can match them up again later.

9 You are now ready to mark and cut the dowel handle using the miter saw. Provided you have followed all the measurements given for this project, the internal distance between the end panels should be 15 in. (380 mm). Cut the dowel to 15¾ in. (400 mm), then lightly sand to remove any rough edges remaining from sawing.

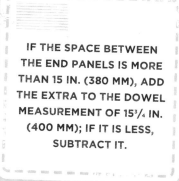

IF THE SPACE BETWEEN THE END PANELS IS MORE THAN 15 IN. (380 MM), ADD THE EXTRA TO THE DOWEL MEASUREMENT OF 15³/₄ IN. (400 MM); IF IT IS LESS, SUBTRACT IT.

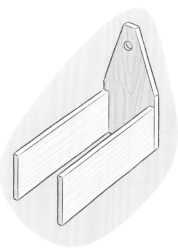

10 Remove one end panel and insert the dowel handle to check that it fits.

11 Take the toolbox apart. Apply glue to one of the side panels. Working quickly, press one end panel onto this panel and then screw the two panels together. Attach the other side panel to the same end panel in the same way. Place the toolbox so that it is resting on the attached end panel.

12 Place the dowel handle in the rebate hole of the attached end panel. Now put the screws into the remaining end panel. Apply glue to the side panels and place the remaining end panel in position, slotting the other end of the dowel into the rebate hole as you do so. Tightly screw the panels together.

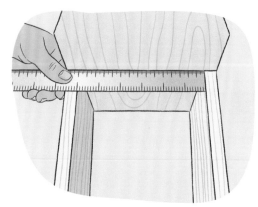

13 Measure the internal distance between the two side panels. Mark this measurement on the off-cut that you reserved for the tool rest in step 2. Cut using a miter saw. Check it is the right width to fit into the tool box.

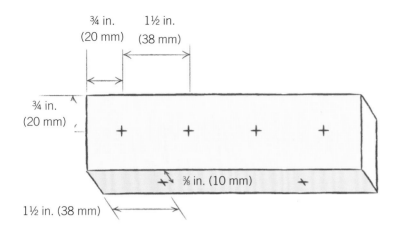

¾ in. (20 mm) 1½ in. (38 mm)

¾ in. (20 mm)

⅜ in. (10 mm)

1½ in. (38 mm)

14 Following the diagram, transfer the position of the drill holes to the top and side of the tool rest.

15 Apply a masking-tape marker to the ⅜-in. (10-mm) Forstner bit, ⅞ in. (22 mm) from the tip. Drill the two screw hole rebates on the side of the tool rest. Using the ⅛-in. (3-mm) drill bit, drill into the rebate holes, all the way through the wood.

16 Place a 1½-in. (45-mm) wood screw in each rebated hole in turn and screw until the screw tip is just showing through the other side.

17 Draw a line across the inside of the end panel at the height of the side panels. Now mark another line ¾ in. (20 mm) below this line. The tool rest will be placed at this line. Put the tool rest in position and push down firmly so that the screw tips mark the wood inside the tool box. Remove the tool rest and make these holes larger with a bradawl.

18 Place the tool rest on a scrap piece of wood. Use the bradawl to start the holes on the top of the tool rest and drill the holes at the marked points with a ⅜-in. (10-mm) Forstner bit, holding the wood firmly and drilling all the way through. These are the holes to store tools such as screwdrivers into; depending on what you choose to put in, you may require a larger drill bit.

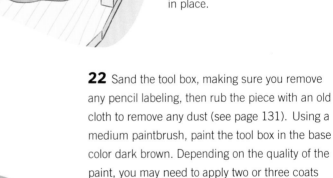

19 Sand the tool rest to remove the break-out from drilling. Remove any dust from the sanding. Apply glue to the base of the tool rest and screw in place.

20 Place the plywood on the floor or workbench and place the tool box on top. Draw around the base; if the box is not quite square, this will ensure it fits. Securely clamp the plywood to the bench and cut using a hand saw. Sand the edges of the plywood to remove any rough sawn edges.

21 Place the tool box upside down on the workbench, with an old towel or cloth underneath to protect it. Apply glue to the bottom edges of the tool box and place the plywood base on the box. Attach the base to the box using panel pins: you will need two pins across each end panel and three along each side. Hit the pins in at an angle for increased strength. Make sure the pin heads are not protruding.

22 Sand the tool box, making sure you remove any pencil labeling, then rub the piece with an old cloth to remove any dust (see page 131). Using a medium paintbrush, paint the tool box in the base color dark brown. Depending on the quality of the paint, you may need to apply two or three coats (see page 131).

23 Randomly dab latex-based adhesive along the edges and on the surface of the tool box. Once it has dried, apply your top coat of white; again, you may need several coats. Using fine sandpaper, rub gently over the toolbox. As you rub, the latex under the top coat will come away, revealing the base color. Do not rub too hard or this will sand back down to the wood. Finally, apply a thin coat of water-based clear matt varnish.

Fleet OF BOATS

Make a whole flotilla of pretty boats to decorate your bathroom. There are two styles of boats to choose from. The simpler straight-edged boat is designed to be cut with a tenon saw. The rounded boat can be made with an electric jigsaw or a coping saw. For the paint finish, you can choose between a stripe and portholes.

YOU WILL NEED:

Materials

Template on page 140

Planed pine, approx. 20 x 3½ x ¾–1⅛ in. (500 x 90 x 20–30 mm); this is enough for four boats

18 in. (460 mm) round dowel, ⅜ in. (10 mm) in diameter, for mast.

24 in. (600 mm)

Thin rustic string: 8 in. (20 cm) for boat with sail; 24 in. (60 cm) for boat with bunting

Screw eyes, two per boat

Water-based paint

Selection of fabrics

Fusible webbing

Equipment

Tracing paper, pencil, and cardstock

Clamps

Workbench

Coping saw/tenon saw

Dust mask

Safety goggles

Jigsaw (optional)

Masking tape (for the stripe)

Drill and ⅜-in. (9-mm) bit

Glue gun and glue sticks

Coarse and fine sandpaper

Medium flat and small round paintbrushes

Bradawl

Scissors

Iron

Needle and strong cotton thread

1 Following the instructions on pages 127 and 136, enlarge and trace your chosen boat template from page 140, then transfer onto cardstock, cut out, and check that it fits your piece of wood. You may be able to cut several boats from one piece of wood. Draw around the template on the wood, making sure that the template lies with the grain of the wood.

IF YOU ARE USING A PLANK OF WOOD, IT'S A GOOD IDEA TO USE THE PRE-CUT STRAIGHT EDGE AS THE BASE OF YOUR BOAT, AS THIS WILL BE MORE STABLE THAN A HAND-SAWN EDGE.

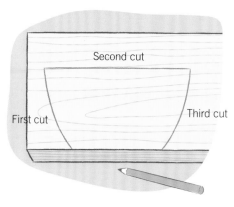

2 Securely clamp the wood to the workbench, then cut out the boat, following the cutting order shown in the diagram. (This cutting order helps to prevent vibration, which could make the sawing more difficult.) If you are making the straight-edged boat, cut the wood with a tenon saw (see page 121). If you are making the rounded boat, use a coping saw or a jigsaw (see page 121).

3 Clamp the boat in the workbench, making sure the base rests on part of the bench so that it does not slip as you drill into it. For the boat with a sail, make a pencil mark on the top of the boat, 1⅛ in. (30 mm) from the bow. For the boat with bunting, make a pencil mark in the center of the top of the boat. Apply a masking-tape marker to the drill bit ¾ in. (20 mm) from the tip and drill the hole for the mast at the marked point.

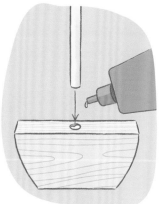

4 Hold the doweling securely on the workbench and cut a 5-in. (130-mm) length for the mast; for this small cut, it is fine to use a coping saw. Apply a small amount of glue into the mast hole, push the dowel in, and leave the glue to dry.

5 Sand the boat and mast, then rub the piece with an old cloth to remove any dust (see page 131).

6 Paint the boat and the mast with your chosen base color. Depending on the quality of the paint, you may need to apply two or three coats (see page 131).

7 Now paint on the details. (Again, you may need several coats.) To decorate your boat with a stripe, apply two strips of masking tape across each side of the boat and carefully paint between them. To decorate it with portholes, trace the template from page 140 onto paper, cut it out, and mark three small circles on the boat. Carefully paint the circles.

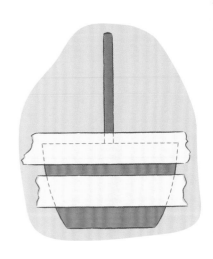

8 Make a pencil mark on the top of the boat ¼ in. (6 mm) from the bow. Use the bradawl to start a small hole for the screw eye. Screw in the screw eye. Repeat at the stern of the boat.

TO COMPLETE THE BOAT WITH SAIL

9 Trace the sail template on page 140 and cut out. Make sure your fabric is big enough to fit the sail. Apply fusible webbing to the back of the fabric, following the manufacturer's instructions. Draw around the sail template on the fusible webbing and cut out.

10 Peel the backing paper off the fusible webbing, wrap the sail around the mast (make sure you leave enough space at the top of the mast to apply the string), and carefully iron the two sides together. Trim the sail to neaten the edges. Heat up the glue gun and apply a small amount of glue at the top of the mast to keep the sail in place.

11 For the small heart on the sail, cut a small square of fabric, apply fusible webbing to the back, fold the fabric in half, and cut out half a heart shape. Open it up, peel off the backing paper, and iron it onto the sail. You can use the small heart template on page 138 from Home is Where the Heart Is if you wish, or draw a shape freehand.

12 Cut an 8-in. (20-cm) length of string. For now, just tie the string onto the top of the mast and apply a small amount of glue from the heated-up glue gun to keep it in position.

13 Trace the small flag template on page 140 and cut out. Choose a different fabric to the heart, cut a square of fabric, making sure your flag template fits. Back it with fusible webbing, draw around the flag template, and cut out. Peel off the backing paper, fold the flag in half, wrap it around the string, and iron the two flag sides together. Trim the edges to neaten it.

14 Now tie the end of the sting to the screw eye. Use a needle and thread to sew a couple of small stitches securing the base of the sail to the screw eye.

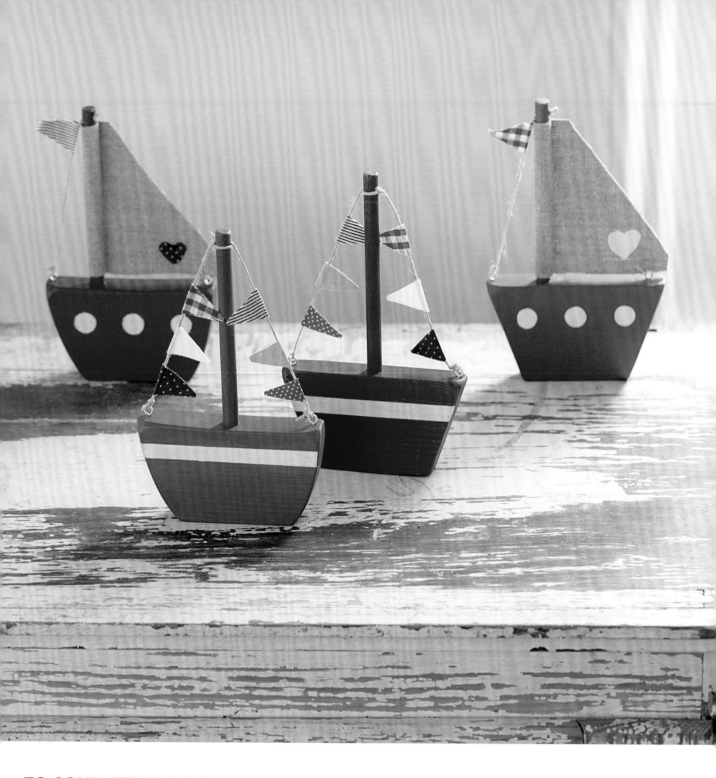

TO COMPLETE THE BOAT WITH BUNTING

15 Cut a 24 in. (60-cm) length of string. Tie the center of the string around the top of the mast and apply a small amount of glue from the heated-up glue gun. Leave the glue to dry.

16 Make six small flags from three different patterned fabrics (see step 13 for making the small flags). Decide the order in which you want the flags to go in. Starting with the flag nearest the mast, attach the flags to the string. Tie the ends of the string to each screw eye. Trim to neaten the string and bunting.

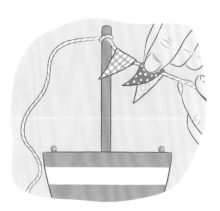

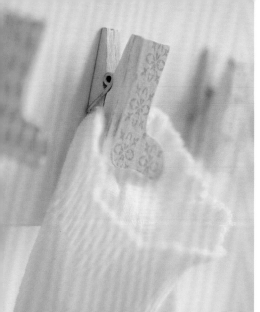

lost Sock TIDY

If your house is anything like mine, there's always an odd sock somewhere! Use this sock tidy to keep them ready for when the other one turns up. I used a different decorative paper for each sock; it's a great way of using up small scraps of paper that I can't bear to throw away!

This project uses a technique that cuts two layers in one go, which means that you cut extra so you can choose the best to use on the project. Mine hangs with string, but if you prefer you can hang it on the wall using mirror plates (see page 134).

YOU WILL NEED:

Materials

Template on page 138

Planed pine, 12½ x 3½ x ⅝–¾ in. (320 x 90 x 15–20 mm)

Two 16 x 3 x ⅛–¼-in. (400 x 75 x 3–5-mm) lengths of plywood

Water-based paint in your chosen color

Five small to medium wooden pegs

Decorative paper

32 in. (80 cm) chunky jute string

Equipment

Tracing paper, pencil, and cardstock

Clamps

Workbench

Miter saw

Dust mask

Safety goggles

Drill and ¼-in. (6-mm) drill bit

Masking tape

Coping saw

Coarse and fine sandpaper

Paintbrush

Hot glue gun and glue sticks

PVA glue

1 Check the wood has one square edge; if it does not, use the miter saw to cut one end square, around ⅜ in. (10 mm) in from the end. Measure and mark 12½ in. (320 mm) from the square edge, along the length of the wood. Place the wood in the miter saw and cut to length.

2 Measure and mark the hanging holes in the top corners of the plaque, 1¼in. (30 mm) in from the sides and ⅝ in. (15 mm) down from the top. Place the plaque on a scrap piece of wood and, using a ¼-in. (6-mm) bit, drill the two holes.

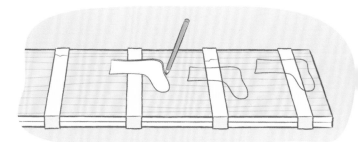

3 Following the instructions on page 127, trace the sock template on page 138, transfer onto cardstock, and cut out. Using masking tape, tape the two strips of plywood together in about four places, then draw around the sock template five times.

4 Securely clamp the plywood to the workbench. Using a coping saw, carefully cut out the socks (see page 121). You may need to re-clamp the plywood as you cut around the line.

5 Sand the plaque and the sock motifs until you have the finish and shape you require (see page 131).

6 Paint the plaque, pegs, and socks in your chosen color. Depending on the quality of the paint, you may need to apply two or three coats (see page 131). Apply decorative papers to the socks (see page 133).

7 Measure and mark the position of the socks on the plaque: the two end socks should each be approximately 1¼ in. (30 mm) in from each end. Then measure and mark the center of the plaque and place the central sock. Finally, place the remaining two socks in position, making sure they are evenly spaced. Each sock should be positioned approximately ¾ in. (20 mm) from the bottom of the plaque.

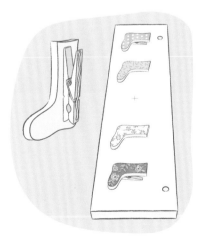

8 Heat up the glue gun. Keep all the socks in the correct position on the plaque then, working one sock at a time, glue a sock to a peg, apply a small amount of glue to the peg, and place back in position on the plaque. Leave the glue to dry. Repeat until all the socks have been stuck to the plaque.

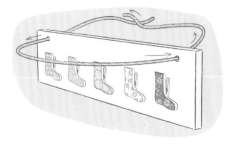

9 Thread the string through one hole from the back to the front, then through the other hole from front to back. Tie the two ends together, making sure that the sock tidy hangs straight.

First Aid CUPBOARD

I have designed this simple cupboard to store your plasters and medicine bottles in; it's also perfect for keeping them up out of the way of little fingers. To help protect the paintwork on the shelves inside, I have applied some sticky-backed plastic, choosing one with a decorative pattern to it; it also gives a nice surprise to anyone who opens the doors.

YOU WILL NEED:

Materials

Planed pine, 40 x 5¾ x ¾ in. (1000 x 145 x 20 mm) for top, base, and shelf

Planed pine, 59 x 5¾ x ¾ in. (1500 x 145 x 20 mm) sides and doors

Plywood, 14 x 14 x ³⁄₁₆ in. (355 x 355 x 4 mm)

Eight ¼-in. (6-mm) fluted dowels

Eight No. 6 x 1¾-in. (45-mm) wood screws

Four 1½-in. (40-mm) brass flush hinges

Two roller catch latches

1-in. (25-mm) brads/panel pins

Two small doorknobs

Water-based primer/undercoat

Water-based satin paint/satinwood

Template on page 141

Equipment

Tape measure

Steel ruler

Pencil

Clamps

Workbench

Miter saw

Tri-square

Dust mask

Safety goggles

Electric sander or coarse and fine sandpaper

Masking tape

Spring clamp

Sash clamps (optional)

Drill and ⅛- and ³⁄₁₆-in. (3- and 4.5-mm) bits

⅜-in. (10-mm) Forstner bit (optional)

¼-in. (6-mm) dowel drill bit and dowel center-point marker kit

Countersink bit/tool

Wood glue

Mallet

Machinist or engineering square

Bradawl

Screwdriver

Hand or panel saw

Tack/pin hammer

Wood filler

Paintbrushes

Tracing paper and cardstock

CUTTING LIST

Item	Number of pieces to cut	Dimensions (length)	Material
Sides, doors	4	11⅜ x 5¾ x ¾ in. (290 x 145 x 20 mm)	Planed pine
Top, base, shelf	3	9⅞ x 5¾ x ¾ in. (250 x 145 x 20 mm)	Planed pine

1 Following the cutting list, measure and mark the wood. Securely clamp the miter saw to the workbench and cut the wood to size. Using a tri-square, check that the cut edges are square. Lightly sand away any break-out from sawing, then label each panel for later identification.

2 Place the two side panels side by side on the workbench, making sure they are labeled right panel and left panel. To mark the area in which the dowels will be positioned, place either the top or the base panel on one end of the right panel and draw a line along the inside edge; do the same on the other side of this panel and then repeat on the left panel.

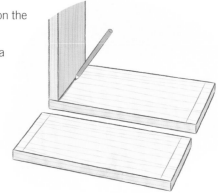

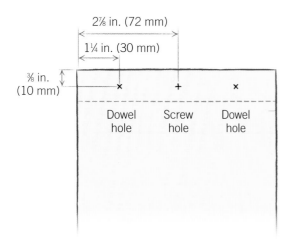

2⅞ in. (72 mm)

1¼ in. (30 mm)

⅜ in. (10 mm)

× + ×

Dowel hole   Screw hole   Dowel hole

3 Following the diagram, mark the position of the dowel holes and the screw holes within the areas you marked out on the side panels in the previous step.

4 Apply a masking-tape marker to the ¼-in. (6-mm) dowel drill bit at one-third of the length of the dowel and drill all four holes for the dowel joints at the marked points. Sand away any break-out from the drilling. Next, place the side panels on a scrap piece of wood and use a ⅛-in. (3-mm) bit to drill through the marked screw holes.

5 Referring to steps 3 to 6 on pages 128–9, make the dowel joints. (Refer to the side panels as panel 1, and the top and bottom panels as panel 2.) To avoid confusion, I placed all four panels together in the correct positions and marked each joint so that I knew which end of the side panel went with which end of the top or bottom panel.

6 Now go through a dry run to check that all the corresponding marks match up before you apply glue to the holes and insert the dowels.

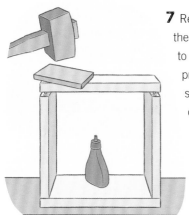

7 Referring to step 7 on page 129, glue the dowels into the holes, remembering that the gluing process needs to be done quickly. Use a scrap piece of wood to protect the carcass, as you use a mallet to knock the side panels into place. You may need to use a sash clamp to finally pull the all joints in tightly on each side. Wipe away any excess glue.

8 To help strengthen the carcass, I always add a screw to each joint. Use a spring clamp to clamp the tri-square into the corner of one of the joints. This will help to keep your carcass square and stable as you drill. Using a ⅛-in. (3-mm) bit, drill through the side panel screw hole that you drilled in step 4 and into the top/base panel. Countersink the hole (see page 128) and screw together tightly. Repeat for the other three corners joints, remembering to re-clamp the tri-square as you go.

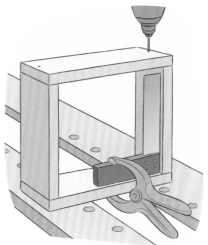

9 Cut two 6¼-in. (160-mm) off-cuts of wood to use as temporary shelf supports. Place them in the carcass of the cupboard and place the shelf on top. Use a machinist or engineering square to check that the shelf is square to the carcass. At this stage, it is possible to alter the height of the shelf. Simply measure the height at which you want the shelf to sit and cut the two shelf supports to that height.

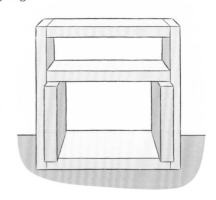

10 To secure the shelf in place, measure and mark half the thickness of the front edge of the shelf. From that mark use a machinist or engineering square to take a line around and all the way across the front face of the side panel. Repeat for the other end of the shelf. This is the height at which the screw holes to secure the shelf will be drilled. Mark a drill hole 1 in. (25 mm) in from each edge of the side panel, on the line.

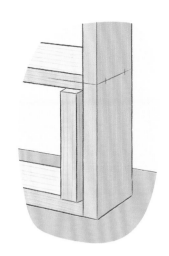

11 Position the shelf flush with the front and back of the carcass. Using a ⅛-in. (3-mm) bit and drilling from the outside of the side panel into the shelf, drill the two holes on one side. Keep your hand on the shelf to stop it from moving while you are drilling. Countersink the holes (see page 128), then place a screw in each hole and tightly screw together. Repeat for the other side. Now you can remove the temporary shelf supports.

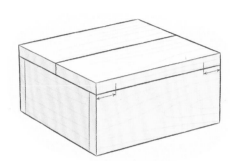

12 Place the cupboard carcass on the workbench, with the doors in position on top. Measure and mark 1½ in. (40 mm) from the top and bottom edge of each door and make a corresponding mark on the edge of the carcass.

13 Attach the hinges to the doors first: place a hinge on the inside of the door, up to the mark, and use a bradawl to make two pilot holes for the screws. Place the screws in the holes and screw the hinge tightly to the door. Repeat for the hinge on the other end of this door, then add the hinges to the other door.

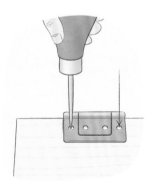

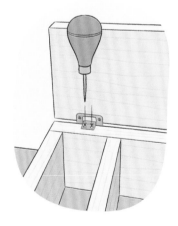

14 Working on one of the doors, open up the hinges to 90° and place the door in position, making sure the hinges are at the correct height on the carcass. Look down the door vertically: you should see a small gap between the door and the carcass. This should align the doors with the edge of the cupboard correctly when they are closed. Using a bradawl, make two pilot holes through the hinge into the carcass. Screw one screw tightly into each hinge and check that the doors will close. Repeat the process on the other door. When you are happy with both doors, insert the remaining screws and screw tightly.

15 Using sandpaper or an electric sander, sand the carcass and doors until you have the finish you require. Rub the cupboard over with an old cloth or duster to remove any dust (see page 131).

16 Put the two parts of the door catches together as if they are holding the door closed. Working from the back of the cupboard, place the catches in position, approx ⁵⁄₁₆ in. (8 mm) in from the inner edge of each door. Using a pencil, mark the position of just one of the screw holes in the part of the catch that is on the door. Move the catch to one side, open the door, and use a bradawl to make a pilot hole. Place the catch back in position and screw it onto the door. Close the door and check the door catch does not rub on the inside of the carcass. Now apply the other screw and screw tightly. Repeat for the other door catch.

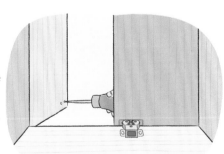

17 Place the other part of the catch back in position. Use one hand to push the door tightly closed and at the same time mark the position of both the screw holes in the catch that is on the carcass. Repeat for the other door catch. The screw holes are often an oval shape on this part of the catch—try to mark in the center of the oval as this will allow you to adjust the catch slightly if the doors do not close properly. Using a bradawl, make pilot holes and screw the catches tightly to the carcass.

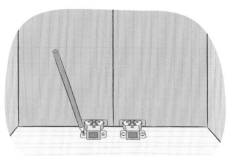

18 Place the plywood for the back panel on the workbench. Put the cupboard on the plywood, with two sides of the cupboard up against two sides of the plywood. Draw a line around the other two sides of the cupboard. Cut the plywood to size, using a panel or hand saw. Sand the edges of the plywood to remove any break-out.

19 Measure and mark 2½ in. (65 mm) from each corner of the plywood and then make a mark ⅜ in. (10 mm) in from the edge of the plywood to mark the position for the brads/panel pins. To help locate the pins into position, make a hole with a bradawl at each marked point.

20 Apply glue to the back edge of the cupboard and place the back panel in position. Using a tack/pin hammer, tap the brads/pins in at an angle of about 45°; this will create a dovetail effect and secure the back panel to the carcass. Use a nail punch to make sure the pin heads are below the surface of the board.

21 Sand around the sides of the plywood with sandpaper or an electric sander to make them flush with the cupboard. Wipe away any dust with an old cloth.

22 Drill holes for the doorknobs in the doors using a ³⁄₁₆-in. (4.5-mm) bit. I placed the doorknobs approx. 1 in. (25 mm) in from the edge of each door and 1¾ in. (45 mm) up from the bottom. If the screw is too short for the thickness of the wood, rebate the screw holes with a ⅜-in. (10-mm) Forstner bit. (Take care not to drill the holes too deep; approx ³⁄₁₆ in. (5 mm) should be enough.) Push the screws through the holes and twist the knobs onto the screws until they are attached tightly.

23 Remove the doorknobs and catches ready for painting. You can also remove the door and hinges if you do not want to paint over them. To hide the screw heads in the side panels, apply wood filler over the top of each screw head. Leave it to dry and then sand the filler down until it is even and flat.

24 Apply primer or undercoat to the whole of the cupboard. You do not need to paint the reverse of the back panel. Leave to dry completely. Apply the satinwood or eggshell paint and leave to dry.

25 Following the instructions on pages 127 and 136, enlarge and trace the cross template on page 141, then transfer onto cardstock and cut out. Place the template on each door in turn approx. 5½ in. (140 mm) up from the bottom edge and centered on the width and draw around it. Paint each cross with white water-based paint. Depending on the quality of the paint, you may need to apply two or more coats. Leave to dry completely.

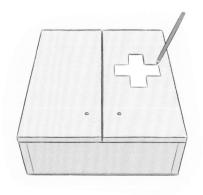

26 Re-assemble the cupboard with the door hinges, catches, and doorknobs.

Chalkboard

This simple chalkboard is perfect for the kitchen or a child's bedroom. Even better, it includes a method of making your own chalkboard paint—which means you can paint it whatever color you like. I love the heart-shaped eraser hanging down; remember to leave the string long enough, otherwise you won't be able to reach around the whole chalkboard when it comes to wiping it down.

YOU WILL NEED:

Materials

Templates on page 137

MDF, 22 x 10 x ⅜ in. (560 x 255 x 9 mm)

Planed pine, approx. 9 x 4 x ¼–5/8 in. (230 x 80 x 6–15 mm), for heart eraser; an off-cut of wood is ideal

Water-based paint, scumble glaze or paint extender, and grout—or blackboard paint (if you don't want to mix your own)

Felt square

PVA glue

Decorative paper

Screw eye

Chunky jute string

Equipment

Tracing paper, pencil, and cardstock

Clamps

Workbench

Dust mask

Safety goggles

Drill and ¼-in. (6-mm) bit

Fret saw

Fine and medium sandpaper

Bradawl

Small paint roller and tray

Small/medium flat brush

When you buy the MDF from your local hardware store, ask them to cut it to the width specified in the tools and materials list.

I cut out a heart shape on the front of the chalkboard, but you could omit this or apply a wooden cut-out heart or other shape if you prefer.

1 Following the instructions on page 127, trace the templates for the chalkboard and the heart eraser on page 137, transfer onto cardstock, and cut out.

2 Measure 19¾ in. (520 mm) along the length of the MDF and draw a line across at this point. Now mark the center of this line. Place the top of the template on this mark and draw around it. Draw around the heart and mark where the hanging holes will be drilled.

Safety
YOU MUST WEAR A DUST MASK WHEN WORKING WITH MDF.

PAINT ONE SIDE
OF THE MDF ONLY: IF
YOU PAINT BOTH SIDES,
THE PAINT ON THE BACK
WILL RUB OFF AND MARK
YOUR WALL.

3 Securely clamp the MDF to the workbench. Using a ¼-in. (6-mm) bit, drill a hole just below the dip of the heart, then drill the two holes for hanging. Cut out the heart using a fret saw (see page 121). You will need to re-clamp often to prevent vibrations and to prevent the frame of the fret saw from hitting the workbench.

4 Re-clamp the MDF to the workbench and use the fret saw to cut the curve across the top of the chalkboard. Sand with medium sandpaper to remove any saw marks and until you have the shape and finish you require.

5 To make the heart eraser, place the heart template on the wood and draw around it. Securely clamp the wood to the workbench and cut out the heart using a fret saw. Sand with medium sandpaper until you have the finish and shape you require. Don't round off the edges—they need to be kept square for applying the paper and felt.

6 Mix your own chalkboard paint (see box below). Apply the paint around the edges first, then lay the chalkboard flat on the workbench and apply the paint to the front using a small paint roller. Leave to dry completely, then lightly sand with fine sandpaper. The paint finish needs to be hard wearing, so I normally apply at least three coats of paint. Use a small flat brush to paint the inside edge of the cut-out heart.

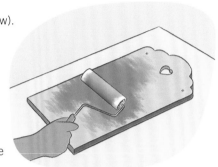

7 Paint around the sides of the heart eraser, using a medium flat paintbrush; there is no need to paint all of the front and back, as they will be covered over with felt and decorative paper. Depending on the quality of the paint, you may need to apply two or more coats. Leave to dry completely.

CHALKBOARD PAINT FINISH

I would normally recommend using an MDF primer, but this mix of paint seems to seal the MDF really well and, as long as you sand lightly between coats, you will get a really good finish.

You will need:
6¾ fl. oz (200 ml) water-based paint in your chosen color
1 tablespoon scumble glaze or paint extender
2 heaped tablespoons tile grout

1 Pour in the paint into a mixing pot (an old measuring jug is ideal).
2 Add the scumble glaze or paint extender and mix together.
3 Mix in the tile grout a little at a time, stirring as you mix. Mix until there are no lumps left.
4 Pour the paint into a paint tray and use a mini roller to apply the paint to the MDF. Let the paint dry between coats, sand lightly with fine sandpaper, rub over with a dry cloth, and reapply another coat. Repeat until you are happy with the finish.

8 Draw around the heart template once on felt and once on decorative paper and cut out. Apply a good coat of PVA glue to one side of the heart eraser and then press the paper firmly into position. Leave to dry completely. Repeat to cover the other side with felt. Use a bradawl to start a small hole in the dip of the heart, then twist the screw eye into this hole.

9 Tie a knot in the end of the string, then thread the string through one hole from front to the back and through the other hole from back to the front. Pull the string at the back of the chalkboard until you have enough slack for hanging it up. Tie a knot in the string at the front, close to the hole; you should be left with enough string to now hang the heart eraser from. Thread the string through the screw eye of the eraser and tie a knot to secure it. Trim the string ends.

Five-plank STOOL

This may look like a difficult project to do, but it is a simple traditional piece that can be made with very few tools. Don't be afraid of painting it in a nice bright color or adding some painted details such as flowers or hearts—try one of the paint techniques on pages 131–2. This is a piece of furniture that should last and will hopefully become a family heirloom.

YOU WILL NEED:

Materials

Templates on page 139

Planed pine, 50 x 8¼ x ¾ in. (1270 x 210 x 20 mm) for the top and legs

Planed pine, 40 x 2¾ x ¾ in. (1000 x 70 x 20 mm) for the side panels

Eight no. 6 x 1½-in. (40-mm) wood screws

Four no. 6 x 1¾-in. (45-mm) wood screws

Water-based paint in your chosen color(s)

Water-based matt varnish

Equipment

Tape measure

Steel ruler

Pencil

Clamps

Workbench

Hand or panel saw

Tri-square

Dust mask

Safety goggles

Electric sander or coarse and fine sandpaper

Compass

Jigsaw or coping saw

Machinist or engineering square

Tracing paper and cardstock

Drill and ⅛-in. (3-mm) bit

Counter-sinking tool/bit

Bradawl

Screwdriver

Wood glue

Paintbrushes

CUTTING LIST

Item	Number of pieces to cut	Dimensions (length)	Material
Legs	2	10 x 8¼ x ¾ in. (255 x 210 x 20 mm)	Planed pine
Top	1	17¾ x 8¼ x ¾ in. (450 x 210 x 20 mm)	Planed pine
Side panels	2	17¾ x 2¾ x ¾ in. (450 x 70 x 20 mm)	Planed pine

1 Following the cutting list, cut the wood. The wood for the legs and top is probably too wide for a miter saw, so it is very important that all cuts are straight and square. Check them all with a tri-square. Label each piece for later identification. You will also need to decide which is the straightest and squarest cut on the legs: this will be the edge that the stool top will rest on. Mark this edge with an identification mark. Lightly sand the edges to remove any break-out.

2 Place one leg of the stool on the workbench. Mark the center of the bottom edge. Set your compass to 2⅛ in. (55 mm). Place your compass on the center mark and draw a semi-circle. Securely clamp the leg to the workbench. Cut out the semi-circle using a jigsaw or coping saw (see page 121). Repeat for the other leg.

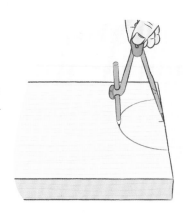

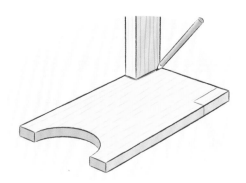

3 Place one leg flat on the workbench. Place one side panel in the top corner of the leg and draw around it. This is the area that you will cut for the rebate for the side panels. Make sure all the lines are square using a machinist or engineering square. Continue the lines up onto the top edge and across onto the side of the leg; these will be your guidelines when you start cutting out the rebate. Draw around the other side panel in the opposite top corner of the leg in the same way.

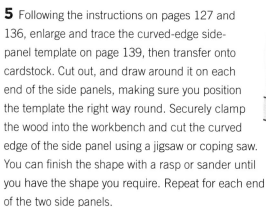

4 Securely clamp the leg into the workbench and cut the rebate, using a hand or panel saw. Check that the side panel will fit squarely in the rebate. If it does not, use a file or a rasp to remove any excess wood. Repeat steps 3 and 4 to mark and cut the rebates on the other leg.

5 Following the instructions on pages 127 and 136, enlarge and trace the curved-edge side-panel template on page 139, then transfer onto cardstock. Cut out, and draw around it on each end of the side panels, making sure you position the template the right way round. Securely clamp the wood into the workbench and cut the curved edge of the side panel using a jigsaw or coping saw. You can finish the shape with a rasp or sander until you have the shape you require. Repeat for each end of the two side panels.

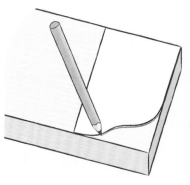

6 Place the side panels down on the workbench and measure and mark the overhang 1¾ in. (45 mm) in from the top edge of each side. Place the two side panels in position on the legs, with the marks for the overhang on the outside edge of each leg.

7 To help mark the position of the screw holes on the side panels, start from the top corner edge of each leg and mark the center of the width. From that mark use the machinist or engineering square to bring the line across the top of each adjoining side panel, then down the front face of each side panel.

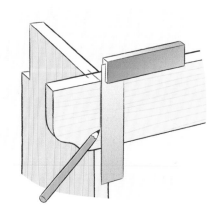

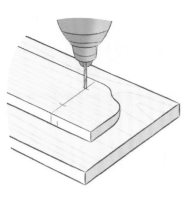

8 Place the side panels back down on the workbench. On the lines you have just drawn on the front faces, make a mark ½ in. (15 mm) from the top and bottom edges. This is the position for the screw holes. Place the side panels on a scrap piece of wood and drill all eight holes using a ⅛-in. (3-mm) bit. Countersink the holes.

9 Place one of the legs in the workbench and put the side panel into the correct position in the leg rebate; if you are unsure which way round the side panel goes, look at the corresponding marks you made when measuring up for the screw holes. When the side panel is in position, use a ⅛-in. (3-mm) bit to drill back through the top hole only and into the side of the leg, creating a pilot hole. (This step is tricky to do, but take your time; after this first joint, the other three are a lot easier).

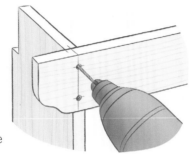

10 Place a 1½-in. (40-mm) screw in the top hole on the side panel and lightly screw the leg and side panel together. Use a machinist or engineering square to check that the leg and side panel are square to each other, then drill the second pilot hole. Unscrew the side panel from the leg and apply a wiggly line of glue, then place the side panel back on the leg and screw together tightly. For the other joints you will not be able to clamp the leg into the workbench, but this first joint will act as a support for assembling the other three joints.

11 Follow steps 9 and 10 to attach the other end of this side panel to the other leg and then attach the other side panel in the same way.

12 To secure the stool top to the legs, you now need to measure and mark the position for the four 1¾-in. (45-mm) screws. Mark the halfway point on each long side of the top, then measure ⅜ in. (10 mm) in from this point and make another pencil mark; this is the position for the screws that will fix the top to the side panels. Place the stool top on the legs, making sure the edges align with the edges of the side panels. Place a machinist or engineering square on the line that was made earlier on the front face of the side panels, than take that line across the top of the stool. Mark the center of this line. This is the position of the screw holes to attach the top to the legs.

13 Clamp the top into position and drill the holes using a ⅛-in. (3-mm) bit. Countersink the holes. Screw the top into position, using the 1¾-in. (45-mm) screws.

14 Sand the stool using either an electric sander or sandpaper (see page 131), making sure you remove all pencil lines.

15 Paint the entire stool in your chosen base color and leave to dry. Depending on the quality of the paint, you may need to apply two or three coats (see page 131). Enlarge and trace the decorative motif on page 139 and transfer it to the stool. Paint the motif in your chosen color and leave to dry. Finally, paint with water-based matt varnish and leave to dry.

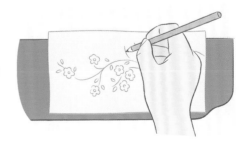

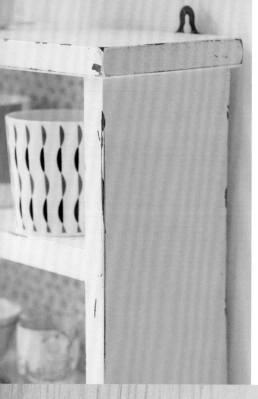

Mug CUPBOARD

After buying a pretty set of mugs, I needed a good way of displaying them—it seemed a pity to hide them away or risk them getting broken. That's when I came up with the design for a mug cupboard. The design can sit on your kitchen worktop or hang on the wall. To make the mugs easily accessible, I have left the front open. I applied a decorative paper on the back panel to add a vintage touch.

YOU WILL NEED:

Materials

Planed pine, 31½ x 5¾ x ¾ in. (800 x 145 x 20 mm) for top and base

Planed pine, 47 x 5¾ x ¾in. (1200 x 145 x 20 mm) for sides, shelf, and temporary shelf supports

Plywood, 14 x 12 x ⁵⁄₃₂ in. (350 x 300 x 4 mm, for back panel

Eight ¼-in. (6-mm) fluted dowels

Eight No. 6 x 1¾-in. (45-mm) wood screws

Four No. 6 x ¾-in. (20-mm) wood screws

Water-based paint in two colors

Decorative paper

Equipment

Tape measure

Steel ruler

Pencil

Clamps

Workbench

Miter saw

Hand or panel saw

Tri-square

Dust mask

Safety goggles

Electric sander or coarse and fine sandpaper

Drill and ⅛-in. (3-mm) drill bits

¼-in. (6-mm) dowel drill bit and dowel center-point marker kit

Countersink bit/tool

Wood glue

Mallet or sash clamp

Spring clamp

Engineering square

Screwdriver

Paintbrushes

Double-sided sticky tape

CUTTING LIST

Item	Number of pieces to cut	Dimensions (length)	Material
Top and base	2	13¾ x 5 x ¾ in. (350 x 125 x 20 mm)	Planed pine
Sides	2	10 x 4½ x ¾ in. (250 x 115 x 20 mm)	Planed pine
Shelf	1	11⅜ x 4½ x ¾ in. (290 x 115 x 20 mm)	Planed pine

1 Mark the length for the top and base on the 31½-in. (800-mm) length of wood and mark the length for the sides and shelf on the 47-in. (1200-mm) length of wood (see cutting list, opposite).

2 Securely clamp the miter saw to the workbench and cut all the panels to length. Label each piece for later identification.

3 Now cut the top, base, and side panels to the correct width (see cutting list, opposite). Using a steel ruler and a pencil, mark the width for all the panels at three points along each panel, then draw a line connecting the marks. Securely clamp each panel in turn to the workbench and use a hand or panel saw to cut along the drawn line. Check that all pieces have been accurately cut and use a tri-square to check the cut edges are square. Sand to get rid of any break-out from the sawing process.

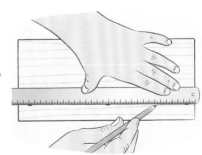

ASSEMBLING THE CARCASS OF THE CUPBOARD

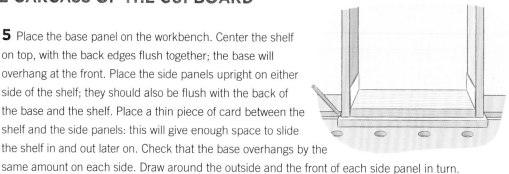

4 Now you are ready to start marking out the joints for the carcass. Decide which will be the front edge of each panel and mark it: keep the neatest edges to the front of the cabinet.

5 Place the base panel on the workbench. Center the shelf on top, with the back edges flush together; the base will overhang at the front. Place the side panels upright on either side of the shelf; they should also be flush with the back of the base and the shelf. Place a thin piece of card between the shelf and the side panels: this will give enough space to slide the shelf in and out later on. Check that the base overhangs by the same amount on each side. Draw around the outside and the front of each side panel in turn.

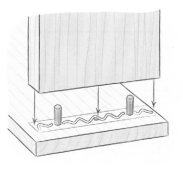

6 Remove the shelf, realign one side panel to the marks, and draw around the inside of the side panel. Repeat for the other side panel, then repeat steps 5 and 6 to mark the position of the side panels on the top panel.

7 Following the diagram, mark out the position of the dowel holes and the screw holes in the marked areas of the base panel. Using a ⅛-in. (3-mm) bit, drill the two screw holes ready for step 13. Now make the dowel joints, following steps 1 to 6 on page 128–9. (The base panel is Panel 1 and the two side panels are Panel 2.) Make sure you label all the panels to save confusion; after each joint is completed, make the corresponding marks for later identification.

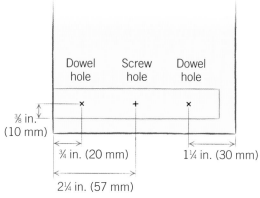

Dowel hole   Screw hole   Dowel hole

⅜ in. (10 mm)

¾ in. (20 mm)   1¼ in. (30 mm)

2¼ in. (57 mm)

8 Repeat step 7 to mark and drill the screw holes and to complete the dowel joints for the top panel and the two side panels.

9 Working quickly, as the glue will dry fast, apply a small amount of glue to the two dowel holes in one side panel and the corresponding holes in the base. Push a dowel into each base hole and apply a wiggly line of glue between the holes. Line up the holes and push the side panel down onto the dowels. Repeat for the other side piece.

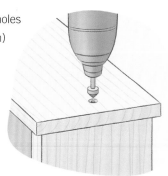

10 Glue the dowels into the top panel holes in the same way. You may need a mallet to knock all the joints together, or if you have a sash clamp, use it to push all the joints flush together.

11 Use a spring clamp to clamp a tri-square into one corner of the carcass. This will help to keep the corner square and stable as you drill.

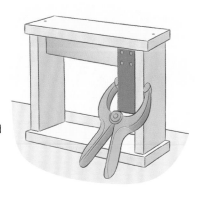

12 Locate the predrilled screw holes from step 7. Using a ⅛-in. (3-mm) bit, drill back down through each of the two screw holes of the base panel into each side panel. Countersink each hole (see page 128), place a 1¾-in. (45-mm) screw in each hole, and tighten them. Repeat on the top panel.

ATTACHING THE SHELF

13 From the off-cut of wood, use the miter saw to cut two 4½-in. (115-mm) temporary supports for the shelf. Place the supports in the carcass of the cupboard and place the shelf on top. Use the engineering square to check that the shelf is square to the carcass.

14 To screw the shelf in place, measure and mark half the thickness of the shelf, then use the engineering square and a pencil to draw a line around to the outside of the side panel. On this line, mark where the two screws will be placed, ¾in. (20mm) in from each edge. Repeat at the other end of the shelf.

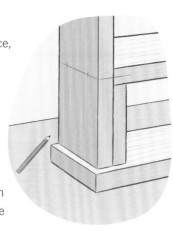

15 Using a ⅛-in. (3-mm) bit, drill from the outside of the side panels into the shelf at each marked point. Countersink the holes (see page 128).

16 Place a 1¾-in. (45-mm) screw in each hole and screw tightly. The shelf should now be secure and you can remove the temporary shelf supports.

17 Sand down all the edges with the sandpaper or an electric sander. Make sure you remove any pencil marks.

ATTACHING THE BACK PANEL

18 Measure across the width of the two side panels, transfer this measurement onto the plywood, and mark at two points across. Use a ruler to join the marks: this is the first cutting line. Securely clamp the ply onto the workbench and cut along the line with a panel or hand saw.

19 Repeat step 18, to mark and cut the plywood to the height of the cupboard. Lightly sand the edges of the plywood, being careful to avoid any splinters remaining from the sawing.

20 On the plywood panel, mark 2 in. (50 mm) in from each corner along the top edge, then measure ⅜ in. (10 mm) down from the edge. Repeat on the bottom edge. This is the position of the screw holes to hold the back panel in place.

21 Securely clamp the plywood back panel to the carcass and the workbench, making sure it is in the correct position. Drill the holes using a ⅛-in. (3-mm) drill bit. Countersink all the holes. Place the screws in position, and lightly screw to check everything is aligned.

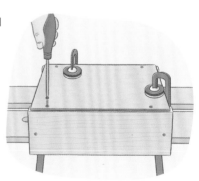

22 Remove the plywood back panel ready for painting. Paint the mug cupboard, using the rustic paint technique on page 132.

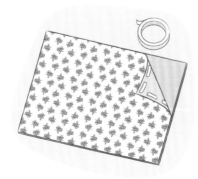

23 When the paint is completely dry, cut the decorative paper to size and apply it to the plywood back panel (I used double-sided tape to keep it in place), then screw the back panel back onto the cupboard.

Storage BOX

This box is the perfect size for storing blankets, shoes, and toys. Slightly more challenging than other projects, creating the laminated lid will give you a real sense of achievement —although you can buy ready-laminated pine boards and cut them to size if you prefer. If you're not keen on the front handle, add a third heart in its place and place a handle on each side instead.

YOU WILL NEED:

Materials

Planed pine, 52 x 7¾ x ¾ in. (1320 x 190 x 20 mm) for front and back

Planed pine, 32 x 7¾ x ¾ in. (810 x 190 x 20 mm) for the sides

Two lengths of planed pine, 59 x 3¾ x ¾ in. (1500 x 95 x 20 mm) for the laminated lid or ready-laminated pine, 26 x 15 in./660 x 380mm

6mm plywood, 25 x 15 in. (635 x 380 mm)

Piano/continuous hinge, at least 24 in. (610 mm) long

Twelve no. 6 x 1½-in. (40-mm) wood screws

1-in. (25-mm) brads/panel pins

Template on page 139

Water-based brown paint

Water-based white primer/undercoat

Latex glue

Water-based antique white satinwood/ eggshell paint

Three 28-in. (710-mm) lengths of chunky jute string for handle

Ribbon/thick yarn in your chosen color

Equipment

Pencil, tape measure, and steel ruler

Tri-square

Clamps

Workbench

Hand/panel saw

Dowel center-point marker kit

¼-in. (6-mm) fluted dowels

Dust mask

Safety goggles

Drill and ⁹⁄₆₄- and ⅛-in. (3.5- and 3-mm) bits

Countersinking tool/bit

Wood glue

Sash clamps

Wood filler

Electric sander or coarse, medium, and fine sandpaper

Miter saw

Tack/pin hammer

Nail punch

Bradawl

⅜-in. (10-mm) Forstner bit

Tracing paper and cardstock

Paintbrushes

Large-eyed needle

CUTTING LIST

Item	Number of pieces to cut	Dimensions (length)	Material
Front/back panels	2	24½ x 7¾ x ¾ in. (620 x 195 x 20 mm)	Planed pine
Side panels	2	12¾ x 7¾ x ¾ in. (325 x 195 x 20 mm)	Planed pine
Lid	4	26 x 3¾ x ¾ in. (660 x 95 x 20 mm)	Planed pine or ready-laminated pine

(If you're using a piece of ready-laminated pine for the lid, cut it to the correct width in step 1 and to the correct length in steps 13 and 14.)

1 Referring to the cutting list, measure and mark each of the panels. You will not be able to cut the wood with a miter saw, so use a tri-square to mark up (see page 122) ready for cutting with a hand/panel saw. Securely clamp the wood to the workbench and cut each panel. Check the cuts are square using the tri-square and then label each panel for later identification.

2 To avoid confusion when marking out the dowel joints, place the panels in their correct positions and make corresponding marks to identify which ends of the panels go together for each joint.

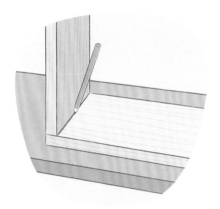

3 To mark out the area for the dowel joints, place a side panel in position on the corresponding front panel and draw a line on the inside edge of the side panel. Repeat on the other side of the front panel and then repeat for the back panel.

4 Referring to the diagram, mark the position for the dowel and the screw holes within the marked areas on the front and back panels. Place the front and back panels on the workbench. Using a ⅛-in. (3-mm) bit, drill the screw holes and countersink each hole (see page 128). Following steps 2–6 on pages 128–9, complete the dowel joints; refer to the front and back panels as Panel 1 and to the side panels as Panel 2.

5 Following step 7 on page 129, glue the pieces together.

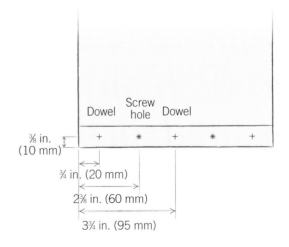

		Dowel	Screw hole	Dowel		
⅜ in. (10 mm)		+	*	+	*	+

¾ in. (20 mm)

2⅜ in. (60 mm)

3¾ in. (95 mm)

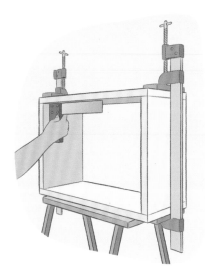

6 Before the glue dries, use sash clamps to pull the panels together. To stop the jaws of the clamp from damaging the carcass of the box, place some scrap pieces of wood between the jaw and the carcass; this will also help to distribute the force from the clamps more evenly. Check that each corner is square using a tri-square. Remove any excess glue. Leave to dry completely.

7 Remove the clamps from the carcass. To help strengthen each dowel joint, place a 1½-in. (40-mm) screw in each of the holes drilled in step 4 and screw together tightly. Apply wood filler to cover over the screw heads around the carcass and leave to set according to manufacturer's instructions.

8 For best results, use an electric sander to sand the carcass. Make sure that all the top edges are flush so that the lid and base will fit well.

9 Referring to the cutting list, measure and mark the length of the four boards for the lid. Secure the miter saw to the workbench and cut each board to length. Laminate the four panels (see page 129); as a guide I placed the dowels 2 in. (50 mm) from each end of the boards and thereafter approx 6¾ in. (170 mm) apart.

IF YOU ARE USING READY-LAMINATED PINE, OMIT STEP 9. YOU'VE ALREADY CUT THE PINE TO THE CORRECT WIDTH IN STEP 1; NOW IT'S READY FOR CUTTING TO LENGTH IN STEPS 13 AND 14.

10 Place the carcass of the box on the plywood and draw around it. Cut the plywood to size using a hand or panel saw.

11 Apply a wiggly line of glue to the base edge of the carcass. Place the plywood on the carcass, ready to tap in the brads/panel pins. Use four brads/panel pins on either side for attaching the plywood to the side panels, and seven along the front and back panels. The brads/pins should go in at a 45° angle. Follow the diagram for positioning the brads/panel pins. Use a nail punch to knock in any brad/panel pin heads that are protruding from the plywood. Wipe away any excess glue.

3½ in. (90 mm)

1½ in. (38 mm)

1¾ in. (45 mm)

3⅞ in. (100 mm)

12 Using an electric sander, sand the plywood so that it is flush with the carcass. The box is now ready for you to apply the lid.

13 Place the lid on the workbench. At one short end of the lid, use the tri-square to draw a square, straight line across the width, near to the edge. Either sand or cut to the waste side of this line to make this end of the lid square.

14 Place the lid on the box, making sure that the edge you have just squared off is flush with one side of the box. On the other side of the lid, draw a line along the underside to mark the length of the lid. Using a hand or panel saw, cut the lid to this length. Sand to remove any break-out.

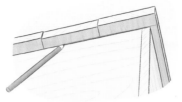

15 Decide which edge is going to be the back of the lid. Measure and mark 1¾ in. (45 mm) in from the edge in three places along the length. Using a long straight edge, draw a line across the length of the lid. Cut along this line using a hand or panel saw. You will now have two pieces of wood: the larger piece is the lid and the narrow piece is the hinge support.

16 Lightly sand the two edges you just cut on the lid and the hinge support to remove any saw marks.

17 Place the hinge in a closed position on the hinge support, with an equal space at either end and with the top of the hinge showing ⁵⁄₃₂ in. (4 mm) above the top face. Use a bradawl to mark the first screw hole, starting at one end of the hinge. Open up the hinge, place it back in position on the hinge support, and screw together tightly.

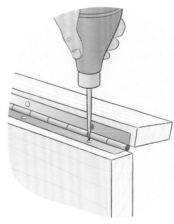

18 Close the hinge again and reposition it so there is an equal amount of hinge showing above the top face. Use a bradawl to mark a second screw hole at the other end, open the hinge, and screw the second crew in tightly. Check the height and the position of the hinge. If you are happy with the position, use the bradawl to mark the central hole and then screw together tightly. The hinge is now secured in place; the rest of the screws will be completed later.

19 Securely clamp the lid in an upright position in the workbench. Close the hinge and place the hinge support on the lid; this time, the top of the hinge should only be showing ⅛ in. (3 mm) from the lid. Keeping everything lined up, carefully open the hinge and use the bradawl to mark a screw hole in the lid at one end.

20 Repeat steps 17 and 18 to secure the hinge to the lid. Place the lid and the hinge support in position on the box and check that the lid will open without catching on the top edge of the box. If the lid does not close or open properly, unscrew the screws and reposition the hinge. Once you are happy with the lid, attach the remaining screws.

21 To secure the lid to the box, measure and mark the position of the four screws on the hinge support. Measure 1½ in. (40 mm) in from each end of the hinge support; this is the position of the two end screws. Now measure 8¾ in. (220 mm) from each end; this is the position of the central screws. Finally, measure and mark ⅜ in. (10 mm) in from the back edge of the hinge support at each marked point. Apply a wiggly line of glue along the back edge of the box; place the lid in the correct position, with the two side edges flush and the back edge of the hinge support flush with the back edge of the box. Using a ⅛-in. (3-mm) bit, drill one of the end screw holes through the hinge support into the box. Countersink the hole and, using one of the remaining four screws tightly screw into position. Check that the lid is still in the correct position and then repeat for the other end screw. Now drill and attach the two central screws.

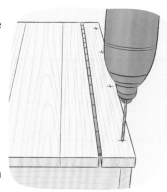

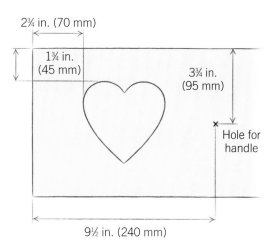

2¾ in. (70 mm)

1¾ in. (45 mm)

3¾ in. (95 mm)

Hole for handle

9½ in. (240 mm)

22 Referring to the diagram, mark the position of the rope handle/handles, and drill the two holes using a ⅜-in. (10 mm) Forstner bit.

23 Following the instructions on pages 127 and 136, enlarge and trace the template on page 139, then transfer onto cardstock and cut out, remembering to transfer the marks for drilling the heart shape. Using the diagram for step 22, position the template on the front of the box and transfer the drilling marks to the box. Drill each hole using a ⁹⁄₆₄-in. (3.5-mm) bit. Sand away any break-out.

24 Paint the box and lid (do not worry about painting the inside of the box) with brown water-based paint and leave to dry. Depending on the quality of your paint you may need to apply several coats. Apply small amounts of latex glue randomly over the corners, edges, and surfaces of the box and lid, allow to dry completely. Paint a couple of coats of white primer/undercoat inside and outside the box and lid, then apply two thin coats of antique white satinwood paint, again inside and outside the box and lid; this makes the paint on the box more hardwearing and easier to wipe clean.

25 Using medium-grade sandpaper, rub over the areas where latex glue has been applied to reveal the brown paint, giving it a rustic look (see page 132).

IF YOU DO NOT WANT TO PAINT OVER THE HINGE, REMOVE ALL THE SCREWS AND THE HINGE AND RE-ATTACH THEM ONCE THE PAINT HAS DRIED COMPLETELY. I LIKE PAINTING OVER THE HINGES SO I LEFT THE LID ATTACHED TO THE BOX WHILE I APPLIED THE PAINT.

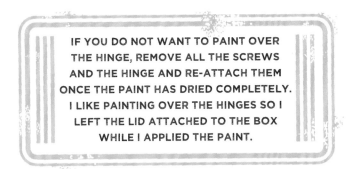

26 To make the handle, tie a knot at one end of the three 28-in. (710-mm) lengths of thick jute string and braid (plait) the lengths together. With a twisting action, thread the handle through one of the holes from the back to the front and then through the other hole from the front to the back, inside the box. Tie a knot at the end on the inside of the box. Trim the ends to neaten.

27 Thread a large-eyed needle with a long length of yarn and backstitch the heart, starting from the dip and making sure you leave enough yarn to be able to tie the ends together on the inside of the box when you have finished sewing. Trim the ends to neaten.

SKILL LEVEL: ✱✱

Tool HOOKS

This project is more practical than pretty and is one that I will be making for myself, as my gardening tools sit at the back of my shed and just keep on falling over. I have designed it so that each peg sits at an angle, stopping the tools from slipping off. The pegs are positioned to accommodate different-sized tools, but if you have tools of a specific size, simply realign the pegs to suit.

1 Securely clamp the miter saw to the workbench and cut the length of planed pine to 32¾ in. (830 mm).

2 Set the miter saw to an angle of 75°, making sure it clicks into place so that the blade does not slip as you saw. Cut the end of the dowel at 75°, then measure and mark 3½in. (90 mm) from the highest point of the angle. Reset the miter saw to 90° and cut the dowel to the marked length. Cut seven more pegs in the same way.

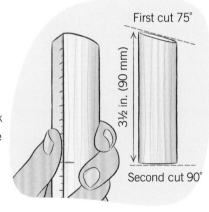

First cut 75°

3½ in. (90 mm)

Second cut 90°

3 Following the diagram, mark the position of each rebate for the pegs on the back panel. Keeping the drill vertical, using a 1-in. (25-mm) Forstner bit, drill the rebates to a depth of ⅜ in. (10 mm). To use the Forstner bit as a gauge for the depth, either apply a masking-tape marker at the right depth or, if your Forstner bit is approx. ⅜ in. (10 mm) long, drill down until the top of the bit is flush with the wood.

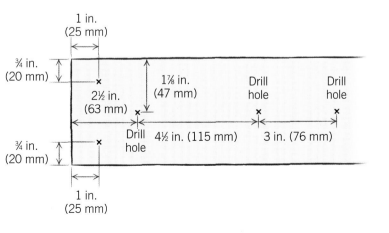

1 in. (25 mm)

¾ in. (20 mm)

2½ in. (63 mm)

1⅞ in. (47 mm)

Drill hole

Drill hole

Drill hole

¾ in. (20 mm)

Drill hole

4½ in. (115 mm)

3 in. (76 mm)

1 in. (25 mm)

YOU WILL NEED:

Materials

Planed pine, 35 x 3¾ x ¾ in. (890 x 95 x 20 mm)

39½-in. (1000-mm) length of dowel, 1 in. (25 m) in diameter

Eight no. 6 x 1½-in. (45-mm) wood screws

Water-based exterior paint

Equipment

Clamps

Workbench

Miter saw

Dust mask

Safety goggles

Drill and ⅛-in. (3.5-mm) bit

1-in. (25-mm) Forstner bit

Countersink bit

Screwdriver

Wood glue

Coarse and fine sandpaper

Paintbrush

4 Using the same diagram, mark the holes for attaching the tool hook to the wall of your shed. Drill these holes using a ⅛-in. (3.5-mm) bit, then countersink the holes.

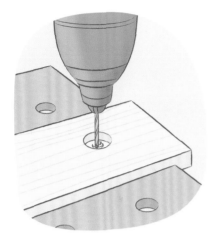

5 Using a ⅛-in. (3.5-mm) bit, position the end of the drill bit in the center of the rebate and drill a hole all the way through the wood. Repeat for each rebate. On the reverse of the back panel, countersink the drill holes.

6 Sand the back panel and pegs to remove any pencil marks and break-out from the sawing and drilling. Do not sand the 75° angle of the pegs; the pegs will be glued into the rebate, so will not be seen.

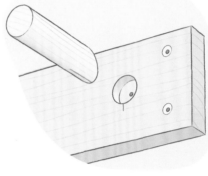

7 Mark a 1-in. (25mm) line at the longest part of the peg and a small line at the bottom edge of each rebate on the back panel. These marks will help you place the cut angle of the peg in the correct position in each hole.

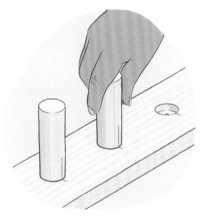

8 Place the back panel on the workbench, apply a generous amount of glue to rebate, insert a peg, and twist it around till the corresponding marks are lined up and the peg feels well grounded in the hole. Repeat for the other pegs.

9 Once you are happy that all the pegs are lined up the same, drill a small pilot hole through the pre-drilled holes in the back panel, straight into the back of the pegs. Make sure you hold each peg tightly as you drill, so that it does not slip out of position.

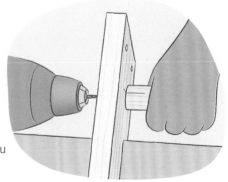

10 Place a screw in each hole and screw the peg and the back panel together tightly, making sure that the pencil marks remain aligned. As you tighten the screw, the peg will be automatically pulled upward, forcing the peg to sit on an angle; this is because you cut the peg at 75°. It also acts as a wedge so the pegs should always remain at that angle.

11 Sand the piece too remove the pencil lines, then rub with an old cloth to remove any dust (see page 131). Paint with water-based exterior paint in your chosen color; depending on the quality of the paint, you may need to apply two or three coats (see page 131).

Shopping PAD

Make this pretty notepad holder and you will never be short of a pencil or paper to jot down notes or shopping lists. It uses a nice mixture of skills and is easily made from an off-cut of wood. You could decorate it by painting pretty flowers across the bottom, or add a decorative paper to the pencil ledge (see page 133), which is my favorite technique. The thickness range given is a guide; the thicker your wood, the chunkier your notepad holder will look.

YOU WILL NEED:

Materials

Notepad, approx. 5 x 3 in. (130 x 75 mm)

Template on page 139

Planed pine, 13 x 3⅞ x ⅜–¾ in. (330 x 98 x 9–15 mm); the extra length is to allow for clamping

Square molding, 3¼ x ⅝ x ⅝ in. (83 x 14 x 14 mm)

26 in. (660 mm) string

Pencil approx. 3½ in. (95 mm) long

Water-based paint in your color of choice

Decorative paper and PVA glue (optional)

Equipment

Hand plane (if needed to plane off tongue and groove)

Tracing paper, pencil, and cardstock

Clamps

Workbench

Coping saw

Miter saw

Drill and ⁵⁄₆₄- and ⅛-in. (2- and 3-mm) bits

⅜-in. (10-mm) Forstner bit

Electric sander (optional) and coarse and fine sandpaper

Wood glue

Paintbrush

Machinist/engineering square

1 Check that your wood is wide enough to hold the notepad. If you are using tongue-and-groove paneling, use a hand plane to remove the tongue and groove.

2 Following the instructions on pages 127 and 136, enlarge and trace the template on page 139, then transfer onto cardstock and cut out. Place the template at one end of the wood and draw around it. Mark where the hanging holes and the holes for the string are to be drilled.

3 Securely clamp the wood to the workbench. Using a coping saw (see page 121), cut the curved shape for the top of the notepad holder.

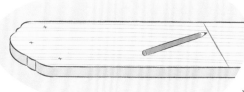

4 Measure 10½ in. (265 mm) from the highest point of the curved top that you have just cut and draw a line across the wood at this point. Secure the miter saw on the workbench and cut along this line.

5 Place a scrap piece of wood on the workbench. Using a ⅛-in. (3-mm) bit, drill the holes for the string through the notepad holder. Now drill the hanging hole, using a ⅜-in. (10-mm) Forstner bit. Place the notepad holder best side down on the workbench. Place the point of the Forstner bit into each hole drilled for the string and drill a small rebate approximately ⅛ in. (3 mm) deep, taking care not to drill all the way through; this is where the knots of the string will sit.

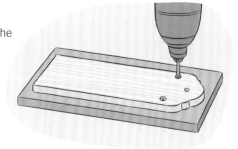

6 Sand the notepad holder until you have the shape and finish you require. You can use an electric sander for the front, back, and sides, but you will need to sand the curved top by hand.

7 Place a piece of coarse sandpaper flat on the workbench and sand one edge of the molding to give a slightly flattened angle. This makes a ledge for the pencil to sit on. Once you are happy with the angle, lightly sand the rest of the edges.

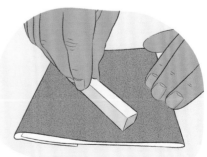

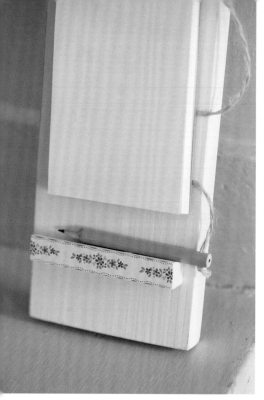

8 If you have chosen to add the decorative paper to the front of your pencil ledge, paint the pencil ledge in your chosen color and then add the decorative paper (see page 133). Then paint the notepad holder with your chosen color. Depending on the quality of the paint, you may need to apply two or more coats (see page 131).

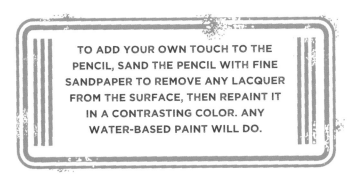

TO ADD YOUR OWN TOUCH TO THE PENCIL, SAND THE PENCIL WITH FINE SANDPAPER TO REMOVE ANY LACQUER FROM THE SURFACE, THEN REPAINT IT IN A CONTRASTING COLOR. ANY WATER-BASED PAINT WILL DO.

9 Measure 1½ in. (40 mm) up from the bottom of the notepad holder and, using a machinist or engineering square, draw a faint line across. This is where the pencil ledge will be. Apply a thin line of glue to the pencil ledge and place it on the line, making sure there is the same amount of space on either side. Remove any excess glue. Leave to dry completely.

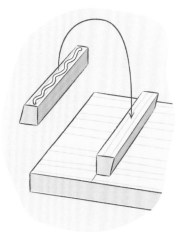

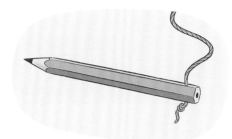

10 Using a ⁵⁄₆₄-in. (2-mm) bit, drill a hole in the end of the pencil. Cut a piece of string approximately 14 in. (350 mm) long and thread it through the hole in the pencil. Tie a knot by the pencil and trim the string.

11 Cut another piece of string 12 in. (300 mm) long. Push this string and the string for the pencil through one of the holes with a twisting action, from the front of the notepad holder to the back. Knot both strings at the back, then pull the strings from the front so that the knots sit in the rebate, and trim. Take the string that does not have the pencil on across the front of the notepad holder and push it through the other hole. There needs to be a bit of slack to make it easy for the notepad to slide in. Tie the string in a knot at the back and trim.

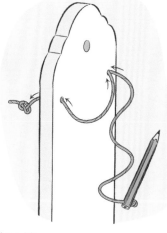

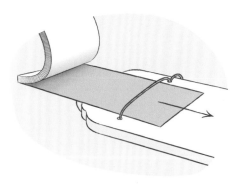

12 Slip the notepad's backing card behind the string, so that the string sits between the backing card and the paper.

laundry BOX

Create a beautiful laundry box to hide those dirty clothes. Your family and friends will be impressed with your woodworking skills, but this box is simply made from four panels that are screwed together. I love the removable fabric drawstring bag, which makes it really easy to carry your laundry from the bedroom to the washing machine!

YOU WILL NEED:

Materials

For the box

Seven lengths of planed pine, 59 x 1¾ x ⅝ in. (1500 x 45 x 15 mm) for the uprights

Two lengths of planed pine, 47 x 2¾ x ⅝ in. (1200 x 70 x 15 mm) for the front and back braces

One length of planed pine, 59 x 2¾ x ⅝ in. (1500 x 70 x 15 mm) for the side braces

44 No. 6 x 1-in. (25-mm) wood screws

Eight x No: 6 x 1½-in. (40-mm) wood screws

Water-based primer/undercoat

Water-based satin paint/satin wood

For the lining

Four pieces of fabric, each 40 x 30 in. (100 x 75 cm)

Matching cotton thread

2¼ yd (2 m) thick jute cord for drawstring

Equipment

For the box

Workbench

Clamps

Pencil

Steel ruler

Tape measure

Miter saw

Masking tape

Drill and ⅛-in. (3-mm) drill bit

Countersink bit/tool

Wood glue

Tri-square

Electric sander or coarse and fine sandpaper

Screwdriver

Paintbrush

Dust mask

Safety goggles

For the lining

Scissors

Pins

Tailor's chalk

Sewing machine

Iron and ironing board

CUTTING LIST

Item	Number of pieces to cut	Dimensions (length)	Material
Uprights	14	25¾ x 1¾ x ⅝ in. (650 x 45 x 15 mm)	Planed pine
Front and back braces	4	15⅜ x 2¾ x ⅝ in. (390 x 70 x 15 mm)	Planed pine
Side braces	4	11⅞ x 2¾ x ⅝ in. (300 x 70 x 15 mm)	Planed pine

MAKING THE LAUNDRY BOX

1 To avoid confusion, sort out the lengths of wood and label each one, stating what each length is going to be used for. Following the cutting list on page 85, measure and mark all the uprights and the braces. Securely clamp the miter saw to the workbench and cut the uprights and braces to length. Label all the pieces.

2 Now organize the wood into four groups: front and back panels (two braces and four uprights each), and two side panels (two braces and three uprights each).

3 Make up the two side panels first. Place the top and bottom brace for the first side panel on a large, flat surface. Place one upright on the right-hand side of the two braces, aligning one of the corners of the upright and top brace to make a right angle. At this stage, the bottom brace is acting as a support rest for the other end of the upright.

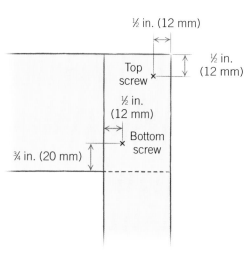

½ in. (12 mm)

½ in. (12 mm)

Top screw ×

½ in. (12 mm)

Bottom screw ×

¾ in. (20 mm)

4 Following the diagram, mark the position of the two screw holes on the upright. Place two screws on each end of the outer uprights and one screw on each end of the central uprights.

5 Apply a masking-tape marker at ¾ in. (20 mm) in from the tip of the bit on the ⅛-in. (3-mm) bit and drill a pilot hole at one of the marked points. Countersink the hole (see page 128). Apply wood glue to this joint, then insert a 1-in. (25-mm) wood screw and lightly screw the two pieces together. Using a tri-square, check that the two pieces are at right angles to each other. Now drill the second pilot hole on the same end of this upright. Countersink the hole and screw the joint together tightly using a 1-in. (25-mm) wood screw.

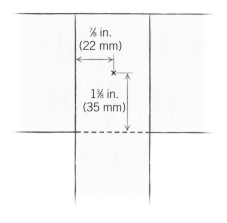

⅞ in. (22 mm)

×

1⅜ in. (35 mm)

6 Repeat steps 4 and 5 to attach a second upright to the right-hand side of the top brace, being sure to check the angles with a tri-square.

7 Now repeat steps 4 and 5 to attach the other end of these two uprights to the bottom brace. Remember to check that the angles are square using the tri-square. You should now have a rectangle.

8 Place the third upright centrally between the two uprights that are already attached. (You can either use a ruler to check that it is central or do so by eye.) Following the diagram, mark the position of a pilot hole on each end of the central upright. Drill a pilot hole on one end and countersink the hole. Insert a 1-in. (25-mm) wood screw and lightly screw to the brace. Repeat at the other end of the upright. Unscrew, apply some glue to both joints, then tightly screw the upright to the brace. The first side panel is now complete.

9 Repeat steps 3 through 8 to make a second side panel in the same way.

10 The layout of the uprights for the front and back panels is slightly different: this time there is a recess at the end of each brace. Lay the top and bottom braces down, as in step 3. On the left-hand side, stand a side panel on top of the two braces, flush with the ends of the braces that are lying down. Draw a line across the top and bottom braces, along the inside edge of the side panel. Repeat on the right-hand side. These lines indicate where the uprights will be positioned.

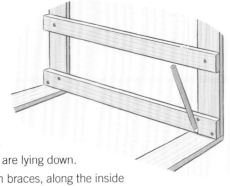

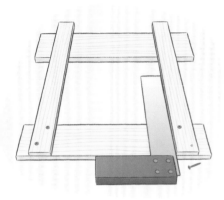

11 Repeat steps 5 and 6 to attach one upright to each end of the brace, making sure that the uprights are placed up to the marked pencil lines, thus creating the recess.

12 Place two central uprights by eye and then use a ruler to check that they are equally spaced. Like the central uprights on the side panels, these only need one screw each to attach them to the braces. Referring to the diagram in step 8, mark the position of each screw hole, drill a pilot hole using a ⅛-in. (3-mm) drill bit, then countersink the holes (see page 128). In turn place a small amount of glue to the joint of each upright and then insert a 1-in. (25-mm) wood screw and screw tightly together.

13 Repeat steps 10 through 12 to make the other front/back panel.

14 Sand each panel. You may want to use an electric sander to make it easier. Wipe off any dust with an old cloth (see page 131).

15 Place a side panel in the recess of a front/back panel, with the braces facing outward. Clamp them both together. There is no need to worry about which is the front or back panel at this stage.

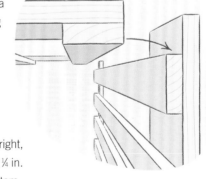

16 Mark the position of a pilot hole on the side panel upright, 5 in. (125 mm) down from the edge of the top brace and ¼ in. (6 mm) in from the edge of the upright. Repeat at the bottom of the upright. Using a ⅛-in. (3-mm) bit, drill the pilot holes through the side panel and into the side of the front/back panel. Countersink the holes. Using 1½-in. (40-mm) wood screws, screw the two panels tightly together. Repeat step 15 for the other side panel, then repeat steps 15 and 16 to attach the other front/back panel.

17 Paint the laundry box with a water-based primer or undercoat and leave to dry. Then paint the box with satin paint and leave to dry. Depending on the quality of the paint, you may need to apply two or more coats (see page 131).

MAKING THE LINING

1 Pin two pieces of fabric right sides together. Taking a ⅝-in. (1.5-cm) seam, machine stitch around three sides, leaving one short end open, to form a sack. Repeat with the other two pieces of fabric. Press the seams open.

2 Pinch in the bottom corner of one sack and manipulate it until the side and base seams sit on top of each other, forming a triangle. Measure 5½ in. (14 cm) down from the tip of the triangle and make a mark using tailor's chalk. Place a tape measure at 90° to this mark and measure across the base of the triangle: it should measure approx. 10½ in. (27 cm). Draw a line across in tailor's chalk.

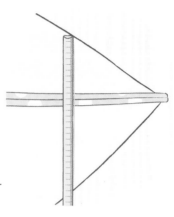

3 Pin and machine stitch along this line. Remove the pins. Repeat steps 2 and 3 for the other corners of the two sacks.

4 Cut off the triangle about ⅝ in. (1.5 cm) beyond the stitching line.

5 Turn one sack right side out and place it inside the other sack, right sides together, aligning the seams. Pin the side seams and pin around the top edge. Taking a ⅝-in. (1.5-cm) seam, machine stitch around the top edge, leaving a 6-in. (15-cm) gap. Remove the pins.

6 Turn the sacks right side out through the gap. Now push one sack inside the other, so that you have an outer sack and a lining. Turn the top edge over to the wrong side twice by ⅝ in. (1.5 cm). Pin and press. Machine stitch close to the folded edge, leaving a 3-in. (7.5-cm) gap.

7 Now mark a line 2 in. (5 cm) below the folded edge and machine stitch along the line all the way around the sack. Remove the pins.

8 Attach a large safety pin to one end of the drawstring. Thread the safety pin into the gap and feed it all around the channel. Remove the safety pin and tie the two ends of the drawstring together.

CHAPTER 3

GIFTS AND PARTY PIECES

This chapter is about having fun and letting your imagination go. You can make simple gifts for friends and family, such as the flower key ring (page 118)—a great personalized present, which could also be used as a bag accessory. I really enjoyed coming up with these designs, so I know you will love making them.

Cupcake GARLAND

Many of the simple shapes in this book can be made into garlands. This cupcake design is very versatile: for my niece, I enlarged the template and made a bigger garland for her garden birthday party. I have also used them as individual decorations to hang on doorknobs in the kitchen.

YOU WILL NEED:

Materials

Templates on pages 136 and 138

Planed pine, approx. 32 x 3⅛ x ¼–⅜ in. (800 x 80 x 6–8 mm); a 32-in. (800-mm) length of tongue-and-groove paneling is ideal

Selection of water-based paints

10 ft (3 m) rustic jute string

8 beads for threading onto the string

Equipment

Tracing paper, pencil, and cardstock

Clamps

Workbench

Coping saw

Drill and ⅛-in. (3-mm) drill bit

Coarse and fine sandpaper

Medium, fine, and extra-fine paintbrushes

1 Following the instructions on page 127, trace the cupcake and heart templates on pages 136 and 138, transfer onto cardstock, and cut out. Draw around the templates on the wood, taking the grain of the wood into account; you will need five cupcakes and four hearts. Using the template, mark the position of the holes for the hanging threads.

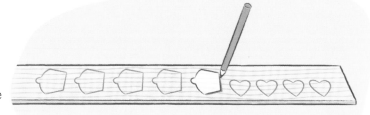

2 Securely clamp the wood to the workbench. Using a coping saw, cut out the cupcakes and the hearts (see page 121); you may need to re-clamp the wood as you cut.

3 Drill all the hanging holes using a ⅛-in. (3-mm) bit.

4 Sand the cupcakes and hearts, then rub the pieces with an old cloth to remove any dust (see page 131).

> THE HEARTS WILL HAVE THE GRAIN RUNNING IN A DIFFERENT DIRECTION FROM THE CUPCAKES AND IT IS IMPORTANT TO FOLLOW THE LAYOUT IN THE DIAGRAM. TRY TO AVOID PLACING THE TEMPLATE OVER ANY KNOTS.

5 Using the tracing paper template, mark the detail of the painting lines for the frosting (icing) and the cupcake cases on the cupcakes; these are your base colors. Paint the frosting, then the cupcake cases, allowing the paint to dry between stages. Depending on the quality of the paint, you may need to apply two or three coats (see page 131); you will also need to paint the front and the back of each cupcake and heart.

6 Using the template, mark and paint the details in the following order: cherries, hearts (as they are the same color as the cherries), scalloped frosting edge, spots on the cupcake cases (see page 132), sprinkles under the cherries (in two colors).

7 Clear the hanging holes of any paint using a cocktail stick. Lay the pieces out on your workbench, alternating cupcakes and hearts and turning alternate cupcakes over so that the hole is on the left and then the right as you lay them out.

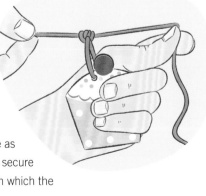

8 Cut approx. 10 ft (3 m) of string. Thread on the central cupcake and move it along to the center of the string. Make the first half of an overhand knot, making sure you do not pull it tight to the cupcake. Tie the second half of the overhand knot, holding the cupcake as you pull it. This second knot should secure the first knot, leaving a small loop on which the cupcake hangs.

9 Place this central cupcake on the bench. Thread on a bead, then thread on a heart approximately 7 in. (18 cm) away from the top of the knot on the cupcake. Repeat the same knot for the top of the heart. Add another bead, then thread on the next cupcake. Repeat until you have completed that side of the garland. Now repeat for the other side of the garland until you have used up all the cupcakes and hearts.

Winged ANGEL

Just as the heart is a symbol of love, the angel is a symbol of protection. I love the thought that we all have a guardian angel to help guide and protect us through life. Over the years, the design of my angel has attracted both adults and children and is especially popular at Christmas: the iridescent wings look great against the lights of the Christmas tree. The technique of sewing on the wings is one of my favorites and always gets people wondering how on earth it is done.

YOU WILL NEED:

Materials

Templates on page 136

Planed pine, 12 x 3⅛ x ¼ in. (300 x 80 x 6–8 mm); a 12-in. (30-cm) length of tongue-and-groove paneling is ideal

Water-based paints

Glitter/fine glitter dust

Laminate sheet

Iridescent foil or patterned paper

Elastic cord (available from jewelry-making section of craft store)

Gold thread

Equipment

Tracing paper, pencil, and paper

Clamps

Workbench

Coping saw

Dust mask

Safety goggles

Drill and ³⁄₆₄- and ⅛-in. (1- and 3-mm) drill bits

Coarse and fine sandpaper

Medium, fine, and extra-fine paintbrushes

Scissors

Laminator

Sewing needle

1 Trace the angel template on page 136, cut out, and draw around it on the wood, taking the grain of the wood into account.

2 Securely clamp the wood to the workbench. Using a coping saw, cut out the angel (see page 121); you may need to re-clamp the piece as you cut around it. Using the template, mark the position of the hole for the hanging thread. (The wing holes will be drilled after painting.) Drill the hole using a ⅛-in. (3-mm) bit.

3 Sand the angel, then rub the piece with an old cloth to remove any dust (see page 131).

4 Using a medium paintbrush, paint the whole angel in a skin tone. Depending on the quality of the paint, you may need to apply two or three coats (see page 131). Referring to the template, draw on the detail of the dress, hair, and face with a pencil. Using a fine paintbrush, paint the dress and hair in your chosen colors. Paint the facial details using an extra-fine brush.

5 Use the tracing-paper template to mark the detail of the dress, then paint it with an extra-fine round brush. As soon as you have applied the paint, sprinkle it with glitter. Tap off the surplus glitter and leave to dry completely.

6 Following the manufacturer's instructions, laminate a piece of iridescent foil or pretty paper. Trace the wings template on page 136 onto paper and cut out. Using the template, cut out the wings from the laminated foil or paper.

7 Using the template for the angel, mark the holes for the wings on the front of the angel. Drill the holes using a ¾₄-in. (1-mm) drill bit. Hold the wings in the correct position on the back of the angel. Push a needle through both drill holes and through the laminated wings at the back.

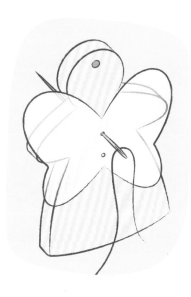

8 Thread a needle with a short length of elastic cord. Working from the back of the angel to the front, take the needle through the first wing hole, making sure you don't pull the elastic all the way through, and then back through the second wing hole. Tie the two ends of the elastic tightly together and trim.

9 Push the gold thread through the hanging hole at the top of the angel, using a twisting action. Make a loose knot halfway up the thread and give the piece a tug down. Tie the loose ends together in an overhand knot.

Garden Party BUNTING

This wooden bunting makes a really eye-catching decoration for a garden party or barbecue; it can be left out all year and is perfect for decorating the summer house, playhouse, or even an old shed. I love having it around my garden so that even on those dull, gloomy days I can see its colorful, rustic charm.

YOU WILL NEED:

Materials

Template on page 136

Plywood, approx. 20 x 4 x ⅛–¼ in. (500 x 100 x 3–6 mm)

8 beads with hole large enough to thread on the jute

Water-based paint in colors of your choice

Water-based clear matte varnish

2 yd (2 m) jute string

Equipment

Tracing paper and pencil

Clamps

Workbench

Tenon or miter saw

Dust mask

Safety goggles

Drill and ⅛-in. (3-mm) drill bit

Coarse and fine sandpaper

Medium flat and fine round paintbrushes

Medium brush for varnish

Wooden toothpick

1 Following the instructions on page 127, trace the template on page 136, transfer onto cardstock, and cut out. Place it on the plywood as shown in the diagram. Draw around the template: you will be able to cut eight triangles from the size of plywood specified. This layout helps to reduce the number of cuts and makes good use of the straight cut edges of the wood for the top of the bunting.

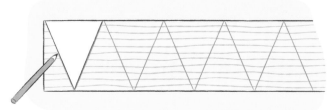

2 Now clamp the plywood to your workbench and cut out the triangles, using either a tenon or a miter saw (see page 121).

3 Place the template on the plywood and mark the position of the hanging holes. Drill the holes using a ⅛-in. (3-mm) bit. Repeat this process on each triangle.

4 Sand the triangles, then rub with an old cloth to remove any dust (see page 131).

5 Using a medium flat paintbrush, paint each triangle in your chosen base color. Depending on the quality of the paint, you may need to apply two or three coats (see page 131). Use the template to mark position of the spots on all the triangles, then paint the spots using a fine, round brush (see page 132). Leave to dry.

6 Using a medium brush, apply the varnish to the front, back, and sides of each triangle in turn, taking care to cover it completely. This will protect the bunting once in the garden.

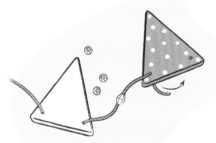

7 Check the holes for the hanging string: if they are blocked with paint, scrape them out with a wooden toothpick. Thread the string through one hole in the first triangle, from front to back. Bring the string across the back of the triangle and through the other hole. Thread on a bead. Repeat, alternating triangles and beads all the way along the string and spacing them evenly with approximately 5 in. (120 mm) between each triangle. Tie a hanging loop at each end of the string.

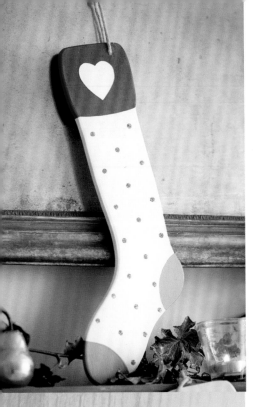

Christmas STOCKING

These stockings add a touch of tradition to your Christmas fireplace, but with an unusual twist. Make a set of three different stockings and decorate them in different ways.

YOU WILL NEED:

Materials

Template on page 141

20 x 8 x ¼–½ in. (500 x 200 x 6–12 mm) plywood; this is enough for one stocking

Water-based paint in a selection of colors

Glitter (optional)

Jute string

Equipment

Tracing paper, pencil, and cardstock

Clamps

Workbench

Electric jigsaw

Dust mask

Safety goggles

Drill and ⅛-in. (3-mm) drill bit

Electric sander or coarse and fine sandpaper

Selection of paintbrushes

Wooden toothpick

1 Following the instructions on pages 127 and 136, enlarge and trace the stocking template on page 141, then transfer onto cardstock. Cut out the template and draw around it on the plywood. Mark where the hanging hole will be drilled.

2 Securely clamp the wood to the workbench. Using a jigsaw (see page 121) and working in the direction shown in the diagram, cut out the stocking shape.

3 Drill the hanging hole, using a ⅛-in. (3-mm) bit.

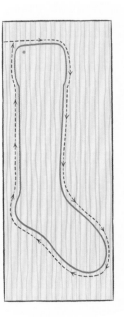

4 Using an electric sander, round off all the edges. Make sure you work in a well-ventilated area and use a dust mask. If you don't have an electric sander, use coarse and fine sandpaper to round off the edges, until you have the finish you require.

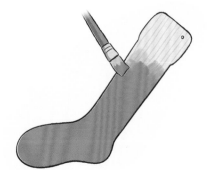

5 Paint the sides, front, and back of the stocking in your chosen base color. Depending on the quality of the paint, you may need to apply two or three coats (see page 131). Leave to dry completely. Check the hole for hanging the string: if it is blocked with paint, clear it out with a wooden toothpick.

6 Make a tracing paper template of the painting lines and transfer them to the stockings (see page 141).

7 Paint the details on the stocking using a fine round brush. If you want to add glitter, sprinkle it on while the paint is still wet.

8 Push the string or ribbon through the holes, using a twisting action. Make a loose knot halfway up the string and give the piece a tug down. Tie the loose ends together in an overhand knot.

Christmas GLITTER STAR

Grouped together, these glittery stars will add Christmas sparkle to your home. They are perfect for hanging on your Christmas tree. This is a lovely project to do with children: once you have cut out the stars, they will enjoy decorating them. Start a family tradition and make a new decoration each year to build special memories.

YOU WILL NEED:

Materials

Template on page 141
Planed pine, 10 x 2¾ x ¼–½ in. (250 x 70 x 6–12 mm); tongue-and-groove paneling is ideal
Water-based paint for base color
Glitter or glitter dust
PVA glue
String or ribbon for hanging

Equipment

Tracing paper, pencil, and cardstock
Clamps
Workbench
Coping saw
Dust mask
Safety goggles
Drill and 9⁄64 in. (3.5-mm) drill bit
Coarse and fine sandpaper
Paintbrushes
Tray/paper for glitter
Wooden toothpick

1 Following the instructions on pages 127 and 136, enlarge and trace the star template on page 141, then transfer onto cardstock and cut out. Draw around it onto the wood, taking the direction of the grain into account. Mark where the hanging hole will be drilled.

2 Securely clamp the wood to the workbench. Using a coping saw, cut out the star shape (see page 121); you may need to re-clamp the wood as you work around the line. Drill the hanging hole using a 9⁄64-in. (3.5-mm) bit.

3 Sand the star until you have the finish and shape you require (see page 131). Paint the whole star with your chosen base color. Using fine sandpaper, rub gently over the star to remove any raised grain. Depending on the quality of the paint, you may need to apply more than one coat (see page 131).

4 Apply a thick layer of PVA glue to one side of the star; the glue needs to be thick to hold the glitter firmly. Generously sprinkle the glitter over the glue, trying to cover evenly. Tap off the excess glitter into a tray or piece of paper so that you can use it on another project.

5 Check the hole for the hanging thread; if it is blocked with paint, glue, or glitter, clear it out with a wooden toothpick. Leave to dry completely.

6 Push the string or ribbon through the hole, using a twisting action. Make a loose knot halfway up the string and give the piece a tug down. Tie the loose ends together in an overhand knot and trim.

Home is WHERE THE HEART IS

This is a design that makes a lovely gift for a new home and brings a smile to my face every time I make it. It sums up my approach to interior design: love your home, make it beautiful, and add a touch of fun.

YOU WILL NEED:

Materials

Templates on page 138

Planed pine, approx. 12 x 3½ x ¼–⁵⁄₁₆ in. (300 x 90 x 6–8 mm); a 12-in. (300-mm) length of tongue-and-groove paneling is ideal

Selection of water-based paints

Water-based wood stain for house (optional)

4-in. (10-cm) length of fine wire

String for hanging

Equipment

Tracing paper, pencil, and cardstock

Clamps

Workbench

Coping saw

Dust mask

Safety goggles

Drill and ³⁄₆₄- and ⅛-in. (1- and 3-mm) bits

Coarse and fine sandpaper

Paintbrushes

Small pliers or wire cutters

1 Following the instructions on page 127, trace the house and heart templates on page 138, transfer onto cardstock, and cut out. Draw around the templates on the wood, taking the grain of the wood into account.

2 Securely clamp the wood to the workbench. Use a coping saw to cut out the heart, then cut out the house. (You may need to re-clamp the piece as you cut around it.) Using the template, mark where the hanging holes are to be drilled. Drill the hanging hole at the top of the house using a ⅛-in. (3-mm) bit. You will drill the other two holes later.

3 Sand the house and the heart, then rub the pieces with an old cloth to remove any dust (see page 131).

4 Paint the entire house in the base color—brown—and leave to dry. Depending on the quality of the paint or wood stain, you may need to apply two or three coats (see page 131).

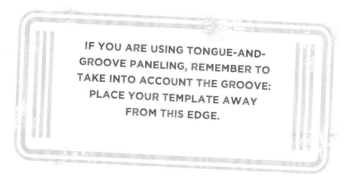

IF YOU ARE USING TONGUE-AND-GROOVE PANELING, REMEMBER TO TAKE INTO ACCOUNT THE GROOVE: PLACE YOUR TEMPLATE AWAY FROM THIS EDGE.

5 Using the template and strips of masking tape, mark out the painting lines of the roof, paint the roof, and leave to dry. Then do the same for the front façade of the house, paint in your chosen color, and again leave to dry.

6 Mark the position of the windows and the door. Using a fine, flat brush, paint the door first, and then the windows. Then use a very fine round brush to paint in the window detail.

7 Using the template, mark the position of the spots on the roof. Paint in the spots (see page 132).

8 Paint the heart in your chosen color. You may wish to add a small flower detail or glitter.

9 Using the template, mark the drill holes in the bottom of the house and the top of the heart. Drill the holes using a ³⁄₆₄-in. (1-mm) bit.

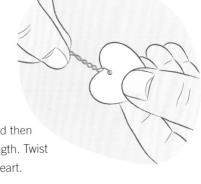

10 Thread the wire through the heart and then fold the wire at about two-thirds of the length. Twist the wire a couple of times to secure the heart.

11 Thread the longer end of the wire through the hole at the bottom of the house. Twist the two ends together tightly at the back. Trim this end and fold it out of the way, so that it doesn't catch on anything. You may want to add more twist to the wire: do this by just twisting the heart (but don't twist too much, as this will break the wire).

12 Push the string through the hanging hole at the top of the house, using a twisting action. Make a loose knot halfway up the string and give the piece a tug down. Tie the loose ends together in an overhand knot.

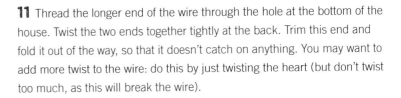

SKILL LEVEL: ✳ ✳

Freestanding HEART

This heart is perfect for displaying table numbers or guests' names at wedding receptions; it also makes a lovely ornament at home. If you have ever tried drilling into the center point of a heart, it is nearly impossible to stop the drill bit from slipping to the side, which results in the heart sitting at a funny angle; this project will show you an easy technique for achieving this. I've decorated the heart with paper, but it would look great with any of the other finishes in this book. Alternatively, use a rasp or a file to create a rounded heart and then just paint it a pretty color.

YOU WILL NEED:

Materials

Template on page 138
Planed pine, 12 x 4½ x ¾ in. (350 x 115 x 20 mm) for the heart
Planed pine, 10 x 2¾ x ¾ in. (255 x 70 x 20 mm) for the base
8-in. (200-mm) length of round dowel, ⅜ in. (10 mm) in diameter
Water-based paint
PVA glue
Decorative paper

Equipment

Tracing paper, pencil, and cardstock
Engineering square
Steel ruler
Clamps
Workbench
Masking tape
Dust mask
Safety goggles
Drill and ⁵⁄₃₂- and ⅜-in. (4- and 9-mm) bits
Coarse and fine sandpaper
Coping saw
Miter saw
Paintbrushes
Wood glue

1 Following the instructions on page 127, trace the heart template on page 138, transfer onto cardstock, and cut out. Draw around the template on the wood, taking the grain of the wood into account. The point of the heart needs to be up to the edge of the wood.

2 Line an engineering square up to the center point of the heart and draw a line down across the edge of the wood. Make a mark ⅜ in. (10 mm) down this line; this should be half the thickness of the wood and marks the position of the hole for the dowel.

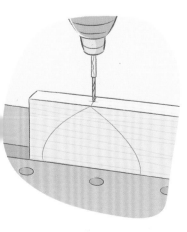

3 Securely clamp the wood into the workbench. To make drilling the hole easier and safer, I drilled the hole in two stages. Put a masking-tape marker at 1 in. (25 mm) on the ⁵⁄₃₂-in. (4-mm) drill bit and drill a pilot hole, keeping the drill as vertical as possible. Then place the ⅜-in. (9-mm) bit into the drill, with a masking-tape marker at 1 in. (25 mm) as before and re-drill into the pilot hole. Sand away any break-out from the drilling.

4 Securely clamp the wood to the workbench ready for cutting the heart. Using a coping saw, start cutting from the center point of the heart. You may need to re-clamp the wood as you go around.

5 Check that one end of the wood for the base is square; if it is not, securely clamp the miter saw to the workbench to cut one end square. From the square end, measure and mark 4⅛ in. (110 mm) along the length of the wood. (The grain of the wood should run down the length of the base.) Then cut the base to length.

6 Draw two diagonal lines across the wood. The point at which they cross will show the center; this is where the hole will be drilled to hold the dowel in place. Use the same drill bits as for the heart—this time, the masking-tape marker needs to be at ¹⁹⁄₃₂ in. (15 mm) on each drill bit. Drill the first pilot hole with the smaller drill bit, then repeat using the larger drill bit, keeping the drill as vertical as possible.

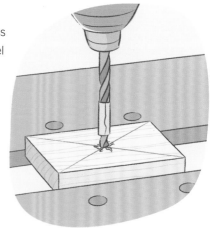

7 Sand all the pieces to remove any break-out from the sawing and drilling and until you have the finish you require. Remember to sand with the grain. Rub over with an old cloth to remove dust (see page 131). Check that the dowel fits into the hole in the base.

8 Paint each piece separately. Apply a first coat of paint, then sand lightly with fine sandpaper to remove any raised grain. Then, apply a second coat to the base; the heart will only need a second coat around the edges, as the rest will be covered by paper. Leave to dry.

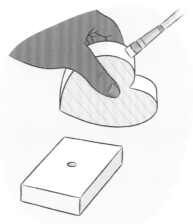

9 Check that the dowel still fits into the hole in the base. If it is a little too tight, gently sand the end of the dowel until it fits. Apply a small amount of glue into the hole in the base and push the dowel into place. Remove any excess glue.

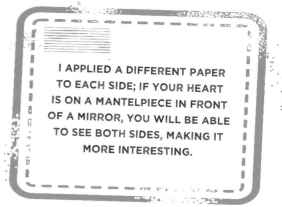

I APPLIED A DIFFERENT PAPER TO EACH SIDE; IF YOUR HEART IS ON A MANTELPIECE IN FRONT OF A MIRROR, YOU WILL BE ABLE TO SEE BOTH SIDES, MAKING IT MORE INTERESTING.

10 Following the instructions on page 133, apply a decorative paper to each face of the heart.

IF YOUR PAPER HAS A SYMMETRICAL PATTERN, TO CHECK THAT IT SITS CORRECTLY ON YOUR HEART, HOLD THE PAPER UP TO THE LIGHT, WITH THE HEART BEHIND IT; YOU WILL BE ABLE TO SEE THE OUTLINE OF THE HEART. PLACE THE POINT AND THE DIP OF THE HEART IN LINE WITH THE STRAIGHT LINES OF THE PATTERN.

11 Apply a small amount of glue into the hole of the heart and push the dowel in as far as it will go. Before the glue dries turn the heart into the correct position, lining it up with the base. Remove any excess glue.

Painted NECKLACE

I had fun making these necklaces! They are simple, quick, and easy to cut out, don't cost a lot to make, and the amount of different colors, decorations, and other finishes you can apply is never-ending. This is a good project to do on a rainy day with the children: you can cut out the shape and they can have fun painting it, then you can enjoy wearing it or give it away as a special gift.

YOU WILL NEED:

Materials

Template on page 138

Off-cut of wood approx. 10 x 3½ x ¼–⁵⁄₁₆ in. (250 x 90 x 6–8 mm); tongue-and-groove paneling is ideal

Water-based paint in your chosen colors

Decorative paper and PVA glue (optional)

Water-based matt acrylic varnish

Waxed cotton cord or ribbon long enough for a necklace

Beads

Equipment

Tracing paper, pencil, and cardstock

Clamps

Workbench

Coping saw

Dust mask

Safety goggles

Drill and ¹⁄₁₆-in. (2-mm) bit

Coarse and fine sandpaper

Selection of brushes

1 Following the instructions on page 127, trace the heart template on page 138 and transfer onto cardstock. Cut out the template and draw around it on the wood, taking the grain of the wood into account. If you are using tongue-and-groove, remember to take into account the rebate in the groove and place the template away from this. Mark where the hole for the cord or ribbon is to be drilled.

2 Securely clamp the wood to the workbench. Using a coping saw, cut out the wooden heart. (You may need to re-clamp the piece as you work around it.) Drill the hole using a ¹⁄₁₆-in. (2-mm) bit.

3 If you are applying paper to the heart, keep the edges square and use a fine sandpaper to remove any rough edges or saw marks. If you are painting the necklace, sand the heart shape with coarse sandpaper to create a rounded edge, then use fine sandpaper all over the piece until you have the finish and shape you require. Rub the pieces with an old cloth to remove any dust (see page 131).

4 Paint the heart with your chosen base color. Depending on the quality of the paint, you may need to apply two or three coats (see page 131). Leave to dry between coats; you can use a heat gun to speed up the drying time if you wish.

5 Choose a finish for your necklace: either paint a flower or follow the decoupage steps on page 133 to apply paper.

6 Cover the heart with water-based matt acrylic varnish to seal the paint and protect it. Leave to dry completely.

7 Thread the heart pendant onto cord or ribbon. If the hole is too fine for the cord, use a loop of wire to help you: bend the wire in half, put the cord in the fold, then thread the wire through the hole to pull the cord through. Add two beads to the cord: one will sit above the heart as decoration, while the other can be used to shorten the string at the back of your neck after you have got the necklace over your head.

Wooden TOADSTOOL

I have always enjoyed decorating children's rooms and play areas in the garden; it gives me chance to play with design and create a magical place. I have a set of toadstools in different sizes around my garden—all I need now are the fairies!

1 Following the instructions on page 136, enlarge the toadstool template on page 142, cut out, and draw around it on the wood, taking the grain of the wood into account.

YOU WILL NEED:

Materials

Template on page 142

Planed pine, 32 x 8½ x ¾ in. (800 x 215 x 20 mm)

Water-based paint in taupe/light brown, red, and white—preferably exterior paint

Water-based clear matt varnish (if not using exterior paint)

Equipment

Paper

Workbench

Clamps

Dust mask

Safety goggles

Electric jigsaw

Sander

Coarse and fine sandpaper

Pencil

Paintbrushes

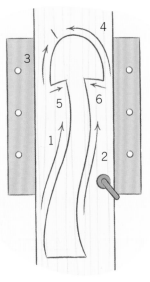

2 Securely clamp the wood to the workbench. You may want to open the workbench as wide as possible and keep the area you are cutting in the center. Cut out the wooden shape using a jigsaw (see page 121). Cut down one side of the stalk and then re-clamp to cut the other side (see cut marks 1 and 2 on the diagram). Cut around the top of the toadstool; this may also need to be cut first from one side and then the other (see cut marks 3 and 4). Finally, cut both straight edges below the toadstool cap (see cut marks 5 and 6).

3 Choose the best face of the toadstool. Using an electric sander, round all the front edges (see page 123). Now check the reverse for break-out and sand until you have the finish and shape you require.

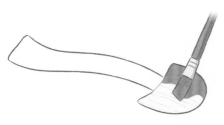

4 Draw a line across the stalk to make it clear where the stalk and toadstool cap meet. Use taupe paint to paint the stalk, remembering to paint the edges first and to sand after the first coat. Paint the reverse of the toadstool, too, as this is untreated wood that will be out in the garden. Leave to dry completely between each painting stage. Use red paint to paint the cap of the toadstool. You may need several coats depending on the quality of the paint. Leave the toadstool to dry completely.

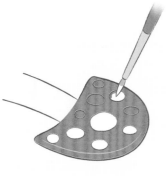

5 Using the template, mark the detail of the spots. Paint the spots white.

IF YOU USE INTERIOR PAINT AND WANT TO PUT THE TOADSTOOL OUTSIDE, APPLY A COAT OF WATER-BASED VARNISH.

Bird LIGHTBOX

The design on this light box can be easily cut out using a fret saw, but you can simplify it by not adding the leaves. The glass paint is optional; I think it's a nice way of adding a splash of color, and the pink and soft green paints that I used give a lovely warm glow when the light is switched on.

YOU WILL NEED:

Materials

Templates on page 141

Two pieces ¼-in. (6-mm) plywood, 12 x 12 in. (305 x 305 mm)

Planed pine, 59 x 1⅜ x ¾ in. (1500 x 35 x 20 mm)

1-in. (25-mm) brads/panel pins

Four no. 6 x ¾-in. (20-mm) exterior roundhead wood screws

One piece Perspex, ⅛ in. (2–4 mm) thick, 10 x 10 in. (255 x 255 mm)

Battery-powered fairy lights, 8–10 bulbs

Four medium-size cup hooks

Water-based paint in your chosen color for base coat

Water-based white paint (or exterior white paint if using outdoors)

Water-based acrylic varnish

Latex glue

Glass paints in a selection of colors

Exterior wood glue

Equipment

Tracing paper, pencil, and cardstock

Tape measure

Drill and ⅛- and ¼-in. (3- and 6-mm) bits

Dust mask

Safety goggles

Electric sander or medium and fine sandpaper

Clamps

Workbench

Fret saw

Miter saw

Engineering square

Tack/pin hammer

Nail punch

Wood glue

Craft knife

Steel ruler

Paintbrushes

Masking tape

Glue gun and glue sticks

1 Following the instructions on pages 127 and 136, enlarge and trace the bird and leaf templates on page 141, then transfer onto cardstock and cut out. Referring to the illustration, arrange the templates on one piece of plywood, making sure that none of the templates is closer than 1½ in. (40 mm) to the edge of the plywood. Measure the distance on either side of the bird to the edge of the plywood to check that it is central. When you are happy with the position, draw around the templates.

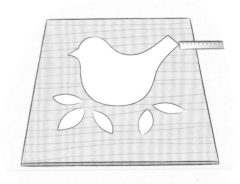

2 Using a ⅛-in. (3-mm) bit, drill a hole just to the inside point of the beak. Drill a hole in each leaf on the inside tip of the leaf. Sand to remove any splinters and break-out.

3 Using a fret saw (see page 121), cut out the shapes. First, cut all the leaf shapes. Then cut out the bird, starting from the beak and working along the belly to the tail. Bring the fret saw blade back to the beak to cut along the top of the bird. (Save the bird shape that you have cut out— you can turn it into a decoration by sanding, painting, and varnishing it.)

4 Sand the inside edges of the bird and leaves to remove marks from sawing until you have the finish and shape you require. This is the front panel.

TO ADAPT THIS
PROJECT FOR THE
OUTDOORS, MAKING IT
PERFECT FOR GARDEN
PARTIES, USE SOLAR-
POWERED LIGHTS AND
PAINT THE BOX WITH
EXTERIOR PAINT.

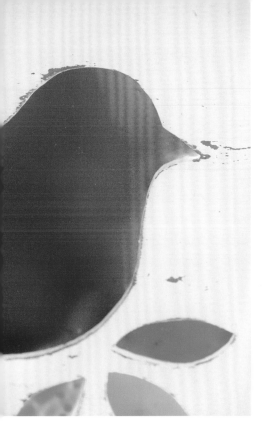

5 Now make the frame on the back panel—this will form a box to contain the lights. From the length of pine, use the miter saw to cut two 11⅞-in. (300-mm) lengths for the top and bottom of the frame and two lengths at 10¼-in. (260-mm) lengths for the sides. Label each piece to save confusion (bottom, top, side 1, and side 2).

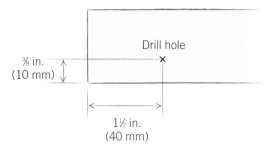

6 Before gluing and pinning the frame together, you need to cut a notch for the fairy lights wire to come through in the bottom piece. Place the bottom piece on the workbench. Referring to the diagram, mark the hole to be drilled on the flat face. Using an engineering square, draw a line straight up from each outside edge of the drill hole and across the top.

7 Place on a scrap piece of wood. Using a ¼-in. (6-mm) bit, drill the hole all the way through the wood. Securely clamp the bottom piece into the workbench and use the fret saw to cut down the lines until you get to the drill hole. Remove the small cut of wood and sand to remove any break-out from sawing.

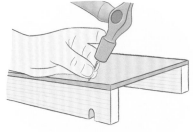

8 Place the top and bottom pieces on the workbench. Working on the bottom piece first, making sure the notch is facing down on the workbench, apply a wiggly line of glue along the length and line up the uncut plywood panel in position on top. (The top piece acts as a rest for the plywood panel.) Tap in a 1-in. (25-mm) brad/panel pin at an angle of 45°, approx. 2 in. (50 mm) from each end. If the brads/panel pins are protruding a little, use a nail punch to tap them in. Remove any excess glue and turn the piece over, so that the plywood is on the bottom. The top piece will be glued after you have applied the side pieces.

9 Next attach the side pieces. Apply a wiggly line of glue along the top edge of one of the side pieces and a small amount of glue on the end that is going to butt up to the bottom piece. Place the side piece on the edge of the plywood back panel and push it up to the bottom piece. Turn the piece over so you can tap the brad/panel pins in, as in step 8. Attach the other side piece in the same way.

10 Now apply the top piece, making sure you apply glue to the two ends of the attached side pieces and along the length of the top edge. Turn over and repeat step 8 for attaching the brad/panel pins.

11 The panel of Perspex needs to be 10 x 10 in. (255 x 255 mm); you can cut it to size using a craft knife and a steel ruler or a length of wood that has a straight edge. Measure and mark the measurements in two places on the Perspex, place the straight edge up to the marks, and run the craft knife down the straight edge two or three times to score the Perspex. Place the Perspex on the edge of your workbench and gently fold the Perspex up; this will force the Perspex to break along the scored line.

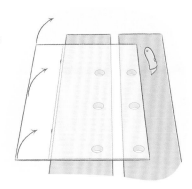

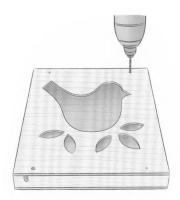

12 Place the front panel in position on the frame, checking that all the sides are flush and that the notch is on the underneath of the box. Now measure and mark the position for the screw holes on the font panel. Measure 2 in. (50 mm) in from each corner along the top and bottom and ⅜ in. (10 mm) in from the outer edge. Using the ⅛-in. (3-mm) drill bit, drill one hole, insert a screw, and screw together lightly to hold the panel in place, then drill a second hole and screw together lightly. With the panel securely in place, drill and attach the last two remaining screws.

13 Remove the screws in preparation for painting. To help the light reflect around the inside of the box, I painted the inside of the box with two or three coats of white paint. I used the rustic paint effect (see page 132) for the outside, using blue as the base coat and white as the top coat. Finally, I varnished the outside of the box to seal the paint.

14 Place the Perspex in position on the inside of the front panel and apply masking tape to each corner; this should stop the Perspex from moving out of position while you paint. Paint the Perspex on top of the cut-out bird and leaves with glass paint and leave to dry. Once dry, remove the Perspex.

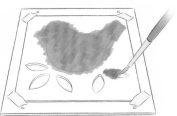

15 Referring to the diagram; mark where the glue is going. Heat up the glue gun, apply a generous amount of glue to the marks, and stick the Perspex in place.

16 To keep the lights in position in the box, attach a medium-size cup hook in each corner. Use the bradawl to start a small hole, then twist in a cup hook so that it is securely in place. Hook the string of lights around the inside of the box, making sure the wire goes out through the notch in the bottom.

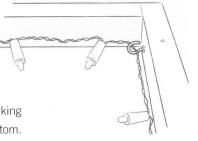

17 Place the front panel in position and tightly screw the box together. See page 134 for instructions on how to attach the box to the wall.

Flower KEY RING

This makes a charming housewarming gift. I have made a whole set in different colors for myself to help identify which key goes with which door in my house. The intricate shape of the flower means that this shape is best cut with a fret saw. It has a finer blade than a coping saw and can get around the tight corners better.

YOU WILL NEED:

Materials

Template on page 137

Plywood, 10 x 6 x ⅛ in. (250 x 150 x 3 mm); this is enough for three flowers

Water-based paint in two colors

Water-based acrylic varnish

Key ring finding

Equipment

Tracing paper, pencil, and cardstock

Clamps

Workbench

Fret saw

Dust mask

Safety goggles

Drill and ¹⁄₁₆-in. (2-mm) drill bit

Coarse and fine sandpaper

Small flat paintbrush

Fine round paintbrush for spots

Flat-nose pliers

1 Following the instructions on page 127, trace the flower template on page 137 and transfer onto cardstock. Cut out the template and draw around it on the wood. Mark where the key ring hole is to be drilled.

2 Securely clamp the wood to the workbench. Use a fret saw to cut out the flower, keeping the blade as vertical as possible (see page 121); you will need to re-clamp the piece often as you work around the line. Drill the hanging hole using a ¹⁄₁₆-in. (2-mm) bit.

3 Sand the flower until you have the finish and shape you require (see page 131), then paint with your chosen base color. Depending on the quality of the paint, you may need to apply two or three coats (see page 131).

4 Using the template, mark the position of the spots on the flower. Paint the spots using a round brush (see page 132). Leave the flower to dry completely.

5 Paint the whole flower with water-based acrylic varnish. Leave to dry completely.

AS YOU CUT AROUND THE FLOWER, FOR SOME PETALS IT WILL BE EASIER TO START A NEW CUT; FOR OTHERS, YOU WILL NEED TO MOVE THE BLADE UP AND DOWN IN THE SAME SPOT TO ENABLE THE BLADE TO TURN, SO THAT YOU CAN CONTINUE SAWING IN A NEW DIRECTION.

6 Using flat-nose pliers, open the jump ring at the top of the key ring finding. Loop the jump ring through the hole at the top of the flower, and close it again.

Woodworking KNOW-HOW

WOODWORKING TOOLS

Having the right tools for the job will not only make your work easier—it will also make it look more professional. This section sets out all the tools you are likely to need and gives lots of useful tips on how to use them.

WORKBENCH

There are various types of workbenches you can purchase; in my workshop, I have a heavy-duty, freestanding bench with a fixed vise, which I made myself when I finished college. I also use a folding workbench, which is easy to store away when it is not in use and highly portable for when I want to work outside. The work surface on these workbenches also acts as a vise, enabling you to clamp awkwardly shaped pieces. All the projects in this book were made using an inexpensive folding workbench.

> * TO MAKE CLAMPING SMALL PIECES EASIER, REST A LONG, THIN PIECE OF WOOD ACROSS THE WORKBENCH JUST UNDER THE WORK SURFACE; YOU CAN REST YOUR WORK PIECE ON THE THIN WOOD, FREEING YOUR HANDS SO THAT YOU CAN TIGHTEN UP THE VISE TO CLAMP THE PIECE IN POSITION.

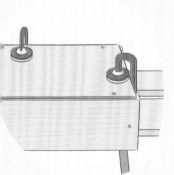

CLAMPS

Doing any type of woodwork will at some point require the use of clamps. It is a good idea to have a pair of clamps, as in most cases one will not be enough.

Quick-release clamp

This is the type of clamp I use most; it is perfect for small pieces and has a pump-action trigger, making it easy to use. I recommend you have at least four clamps for some of the more complicated projects in this book.

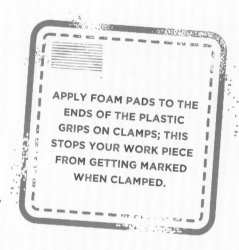

> APPLY FOAM PADS TO THE ENDS OF THE PLASTIC GRIPS ON CLAMPS; THIS STOPS YOUR WORK PIECE FROM GETTING MARKED WHEN CLAMPED.

Sash clamp

This type of clamp is used for clamping jointed carcasses and laminated panels (see page 129) while glue dries. It has two jaws on a steel bar. One jaw is free to move up and down the steel bar, allowing you to adjust the length of clamping; it is secured in place by inserting a metal pin in any one of the holes along the bar. The other jaw has two parts to it: one part is fixed in place to the end of the bar and the other part is adjustable, allowing you to tightly clamp your work together.

Spring clamp

In a spring clamp, the pressure in between the jaws is applied by a steel spring, which cannot be tightened up. Spring clamps are very good for holding tools or wood in position when you need that extra hand.

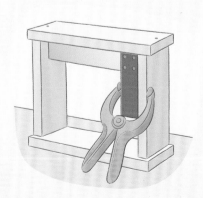

SAWS

Saws comes in many different shapes and sizes, so make sure you use the right one for the job.

Hand saw

There are various types of hand saw used for making straight cuts in larger pieces of wood: I recommend a panel saw, which has much finer teeth, giving a clean cut edge. It is perfect for using with soft wood, such as pine. It also works well with man-made boards such as plywood.

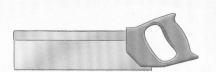

Tenon saw

This general-purpose hand saw has a steel or brass strip across the top of the blade, which strengthens the saw blade. The teeth are small and fine, giving a nice clean cut—ideal for cutting small straight cuts for making joints.

✳ IF YOU FIND IT STARTS TO GET DIFFICULT TO SAW, THIS IS PROBABLY BECAUSE THE CUT IN THE WOOD IS CLOSING IN TOGETHER AND BINDING ONTO THE SAW. SIMPLY PLACE A WOODEN WEDGE IN THE CUT TO KEEP IT OPEN, FREEING UP THE SAW BLADE.

✳ NEVER USE A SAW WITH BLUNT TEETH, AS YOU ARE AT GREAT RISK OF HARMING YOURSELF: IF THE TEETH ARE BLUNT YOU WILL NATURALLY PUT MORE PRESSURE ON THE SAW BLADE, GIVING YOU LESS CONTROL OVER THE SAW.

Basic sawing techniques for panel/hand and tenon saws

1 Secure your wood to the workbench with clamps, spacing them evenly along the length of the wood.

2 Grip the handle and extend your index finger out along the top of the handle (there is normally a rebate there for your finger to sit in). This gives you greater control over the blade while sawing.

3 Place the saw blade on the waste side of the line. Use the knuckle of the thumb of your non-cutting hand to steady the blade as you make your first cuts, removing it as soon as a small cut has begun. Then use this hand to hold onto the wood. Keep all your fingers tucked out of the way of the blade.

4 Pull the saw back toward you, do a couple of short strokes to start with, then use the full length of the saw blade and slow, steady strokes; this gives you more control over the saw. Keep the edge of the saw blade at about 45º to the surface of the wood and apply only a small amount of pressure on the blade. Keep checking the saw blade is staying to the line, both vertically and horizontally.

5 As you come to the end of sawing, support the off-cut in your free hand and slowly, gently, and with less pressure, let the saw cut the last remaining bit of wood.

Manual miter saw

This is a very useful saw to have in your toolkit; it enables you to saw straight, accurate cuts and angles of varying degrees. The blades have small, fine teeth, giving a nice, clean cut. Always follow the manufacturer's instructions when setting up a miter saw.

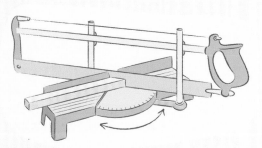

1 Rotate the saw to the desired angle and lock it in place, then make the cut. Place your wood flush up against the back fence of the miter box and hold it there tightly while sawing with the other hand. Move the saw back and forth over your wood, keeping the blade horizontal and applying a small amount of pressure.

2 As you near the end of sawing, slow down and apply less pressure. Allow the blade to gently cut the last bit; this will help to reduce the risk of the wood splitting and breaking off at the end.

Coping and fret saws

A coping saw is a small hand saw, used for cutting out curves or intricate shapes and internal sawing (cutting out a shape within another shape) in thin wood or man-made boards. It has a long, thin blade that has a pin at each end; these pins sit between a sprung metal frame, which creates tension on the blade. The handle is turned clockwise or counterclockwise to release or tighten the tension.

A fret saw is similar to a coping saw, but the blade is much finer, enabling you to cut even more intricate shapes. You can also cut more deeply, due to the extra depth of the metal frame. The blade is in a fixed position—so to change direction when sawing, rotate the whole saw while holding the handle, to keep the front of the blade facing in the direction you want it to go.

Using a coping saw or a fret saw

Place the blade on the waste side of the line. To start a cut, make a couple of backward strokes until you have a small cut. Apply a little force down onto the wood as it saws. You should feel some friction between the blade and the wood. Keep the saw vertical while sawing.

For internal cuts, release the blade, drill a hole all the way through your wood, insert the blade through the hole, and then attach the blade back on the saw frame. When you attach the blade, make sure that the teeth are pointing toward you, to ensure that the cut is on the backward stroke.

Jigsaw

This is an electric hand saw with a blade that moves up and down within a flat, metal base plate. You can change the blades for different tasks; the angle of the base plate can also be changed, enabling you to cut a beveled edge. Refer to the manufacturer's instructions for changing blades and other settings for your jigsaw.

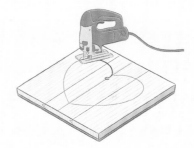

1 Always clamp your work piece down securely to the workbench. Do a safety check on your jigsaw blade before using, if you have not used it for a while. Before plugging into the mains, check the blade is tightly fixed in place and that the blade is not blunt.

2 When you are ready, line up the front of the blade with the line you need to cut, making sure that the blade does not touch the wood. Press the trigger to start up the jigsaw, then slowly move the jigsaw forward so that the blade starts to cut as it touches the wood.

3 Hold the jigsaw firmly, keeping the base plate flat on the work surface, and follow the line. If you start to veer off the line, don't stop the jigsaw; instead, carefully and slowly slide the jigsaw blade back to where it started to veer away and then slowly let the blade start to cut on the line again.

MEASURING AND MARKING TOOLS

Measuring and marking is the most important stage of any woodworking project; time spent at this stage will save you a lot of heartache later on if you've got your measurements wrong. The tools mentioned here are designed to help make the job easier; again, go for quality. As the saying goes, "measure twice and cut once."

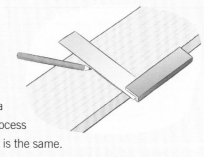

Tri-square and machinist/engineering square

A tri-square helps you to mark out right angles on your wood and is also good for checking that your end cuts are square, both vertically and horizontally. It has a hardwood handle with a brass face; the blade, which is made of steel, is what you place across the wood and mark your right angle from.

A machinist or engineering square is made entirely of metal and is very useful for small projects; it comes in a variety of different sizes.

Marking and checking right angles

Whether you're using a tri-square or a machinist/engineering square, the process of marking and checking right angles is the same.

To mark a right angle, place the square on your work with the handle flush with the edge of the wood, and draw a line along the blade.

To check that a carcass is square, simply place the square in one corner, inside the carcass, and push it up against the sides. If there is no gap between the wood and the blade, you have a perfect right angle; if there is a gap, then it is out of square. It is very important to check that your carcass is square while you are assembling it; once the glue has dried, there is not much you can do about it.

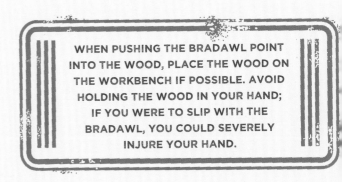

Bradawl

A bradawl, which has a hardwood handle and a long steel spiked tip, is used to mark the position of pilot holes for small screws and panel pins and to mark out the center point for drilling.

Mark with a pencil where the hole is going to be. Push the point of the bradawl onto the mark and twist the bradawl round to enlarge the hole, then place the tip of the screw or drill bit into the hole; this will stop the drill bit from slipping out of position.

> WHEN PUSHING THE BRADAWL POINT INTO THE WOOD, PLACE THE WOOD ON THE WORKBENCH IF POSSIBLE. AVOID HOLDING THE WOOD IN YOUR HAND; IF YOU WERE TO SLIP WITH THE BRADAWL, YOU COULD SEVERELY INJURE YOUR HAND.

Steel ruler

A steel ruler is another must for any toolbox as—unlike wooden or plastic rulers—it cannot get damaged. Make sure that the measurements start from the very edge of the ruler; I find this makes measuring more accurate, especially for internal measuring.

Retractable tape measure

The advantage of a retractable tape measure over a steel rule is that it is longer. The hook at the end is slightly loose to enable movement for taking either internal or external measurements.

TOOLS FOR SANDING AND REMOVING EXCESS WOOD

There are lots of different tools for shaping wood, but the ones I have mentioned in this book are really all you need.

Rasps and files

These tools are designed for shaping wood; they both come in various sizes and profiles (flat, curved, or round). A rasp is the coarser of the two and removes more of the waste wood quicker, but it leaves a very rough finish, which takes more effort to smooth out. A file is much finer and is very useful for smoothing off rough edges that have been made from the rasp or other tools. If the rasp or file gets clogged up, use a fine wire brush to remove the trapped wood fibers.

1 Depending on the size of the piece, either clamp your piece to the workbench or hold it tightly in your hand. If you do have to hold the piece in your hand, I recommend you wear a suitable pair of craftsman's gloves to protect yourself from injury.

2 Hold the handle of the rasp or file firmly in one hand. If you have two hands free, place your free hand at the other end of the file or rasp; this will help steady the rasp or file and allow you to apply even pressure on the wood as you work. Start with light strokes, applying greater downward pressure as you remove more wood.

Hand plane

This is another tool for removing excess wood. I suggest you buy a smoothing plane, which is a medium-size, general-purpose plane. The depth of the blade can be adjusted, allowing you to increase or decrease the amount of wood shaved off with each stroke.

1 Before planing your work piece, check that the plane is set up correctly and test it on a scrap piece of wood. You may find that it planes too much wood away; this will have saved you from ruining your work piece and gives you chance to set the cutting depth of the blade properly.

2 To adjust the depth of the blade, look down the base of the plane: you should just see the blade protruding out. Turn the adjustment wheel—you will see the blade either retracting or extending outward. Experiment on your scrap piece until you are happy with the depth of the blade.

3 Either clamp your piece onto the workbench or use a stop on the workbench to rest your piece against; this allows you to have both hands free for planing. Grip the back handle with one hand and hold the front round handle with the other. Hold the plane so that the base is flat on your work piece, apply an even amount of pressure to the front and back of the plane, and slowly push the plane forward over your work. When you pull back, release the pressure applied on the wood.

TO MAKE PLANING EASIER, RUB SOME CANDLE WAX OVER THE BASE OF THE PLANE; THIS REDUCES THE FRICTION BETWEEN THE BASE AND THE WOOD. ALWAYS PLANE WITH THE GRAIN OF THE WOOD.

Power sanders

There are two types of sander—orbital sanders and belt sanders. Orbital sanders are easier to use and work by applying a sheet of sandpaper to a vibrating base plate; some vibrate with a circular motion. A belt sander removes waste wood more quickly; it works through a continuous belt of sandpaper being turned in the same direction by a motor. Both types of sander come in different sizes and can be fitted with different grades of sandpaper.

POWER TOOL HEALTH AND SAFETY

* ALWAYS WEAR THE APPROPRIATE SAFETY WEAR.

* NEVER WEAR LOOSE CLOTHING, WHICH CAN GET CAUGHT UP IN MACHINERY.

* KEEP LONG HAIR TIED UP.

* CHECK YOUR POWER TOOL BEFORE PLUGGING IT INTO THE MAINS. MAKE SURE THAT THE ELECTRIC CABLE IS INTACT AND HAS NO BARE WIRES, THAT ANY BLADES ARE SECURE, AND THAT SANDING PADS ARE SECURED PROPERLY IN PLACE.

* TUCK WIRE CABLES AWAY FROM WHERE YOU ARE WORKING.

* ALWAYS FOLLOW THE MANUFACTURER'S INSTRUCTIONS.

HAMMERS

A hammer is a must for any toolbox; in all the projects in this book that use a hammer, I have suggested which hammer I recommend.

Claw hammer

A claw hammer is used to drive in nails with the flat head and to remove them with the claw.

Tack/pin hammer

The tack/pin hammer is a lightweight hammer and is designed for driving in panel pins. The tapered end allows you to start striking the pin head without catching your fingers. Once the pin is in the wood, turn the hammer over and use the flat end to finish driving in the pin.

Nail punch or setter

This tool has a small cupped end in which the nail head sits, allowing you to drive in the heads of brad/panel pins and nails so that they do not protrude above the wood. Various sizes are available. Once you've driven in the nail head, apply wood filler putty over the top to fill in and conceal the head.

Mallet

Mallets are designed to help with the assembly of carcasses, joints and for using with chisels. The head of the mallet has two large, flat faces, which help to spread out the impact on the wood, thus reducing damage to your work piece.

> TO AVOID MARKING THE SURFACE OF THE WORK PIECE WITH THE MALLET, IT IS A GOOD IDEA TO PLACE A SCRAP PIECE OF WOOD ON THE SURFACE WHERE YOU ARE STRIKING.

DRILLS AND BITS

There are so many different makes and types of drill that it can be difficult to know which one to buy. I recommend you buy a medium-priced drill that has a hammer drill setting as well as other general settings; this is a good multi-purpose drill that will save you from having to buy two different drills.

To go with your drill, you will need a range of bits in different diameters. Always use the right size and the type of drill bit for the job.

General-purpose bits

Standard twist drill or HSS (high-speed steel) are good general-purpose drill bits for wood, plastic, and metal; you can buy twist drill sets that have a range of diameters.

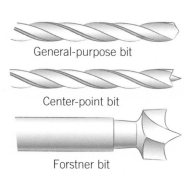

General-purpose bit

Center-point bit

Forstner bit

Center-point bit

This has a sharp point at the tip, which locates the end of the drill bit exactly where you want to drill the hole; it also prevents the drill bit from slipping. There is a smaller range of diameters than for general-purpose bits, but they are perfectly designed to fit wooden dowels for jointing.

Forstner bit

This is perfect for drilling rebates for inserting dowels or recessing screw heads. There is a good range of diameters; the ones I use the most are the ⅜-in. (10-mm) and the 1-in. (25-mm).

> FOR DRILLING TO A SPECIFIC DEPTH, APPLY A SMALL PIECE OF MASKING TAPE TO THE DRILL BIT TO MARK THE DEPTH TO WHICH YOU WISH TO DRILL.

Countersink tool/bit

This tool either comes as a small handheld tool or as a separate bit that attaches to your drill. It is used to create a tapered recess for a screw head to fit in, allowing the screw head to sit flush with the wood. Always drill the screw hole first and then countersink the hole (see page 128).

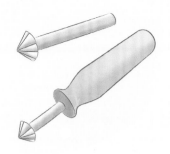

Dowel center-point sets

This is a set containing a drill bit, center-point markers, and wooden fluted dowels that you can buy from most hardware stores. It is used for joining wood, either for butt joints or for edge-to-edge joining (laminating panels)—see pages 128–9.

OTHER USEFUL EQUIPMENT

Scissors

For cutting templates.

Pencil

For marking wood and drawing from templates.

Sandpaper

Sandpaper is essential for sanding away saw marks, rounding off edges, and sanding away raised wood fibers from painting. Sandpaper is graded to show how coarse or fine the grit is. The range is shown in numbers:

Very coarse—50–60 grit
Coarse—80–100 grit
Medium—120–280 grit
Fine—220–280 grit
Very fine—320–600 grit

You will probably find that you will never need to use the very coarse or the very fine.

• Always sand with the grain of the wood.
• Start with coarse sandpaper, then smooth off with medium and fine sandpaper.
• Take time and care when you are sanding, as the sanding will affect the final paint finish.

Old cloths

After you have sanded down, wipe off any dust with an old cloth. It's these little steps that can make all the difference to the final paint finish.

Dust mask

A dust mask must be worn when you are using power tools or even sanding by hand. Make sure you buy the correct one: the packaging should tell you what kind of work you can carry out with that dust mask.

Safety goggles

These should always be worn when using power tools, to protect your eyes from flying sawdust or splinters of wood.

Ear protectors

Protect your ears from the noise created by power tools such as jigsaws and electric sanders. Exposure over a long period of time can cause long-term hearing damage.

Adhesives

For this book, you will need to use glue to bond joints together. I have suggested using PVA, which starts off white but dries clear. The drying time can vary depending on the room temperature: the initial bond is normally ten minutes but it is best to leave the glue to dry thoroughly. For any projects made for outside or areas where there is a lot of moisture, use exterior PVA glue. PVA is a water-based glue, so use warm water to wash or wipe away any excess glue.

Glue gun (hot-melt glue gun)

A cylindrical stick of glue is inserted into the gun; when you pull the trigger, the glue comes out through a nozzle that has been heated to a very high temperature. You need to work quickly, as the glue sets in seconds.

BUYING AND STORING WOOD

Selecting your wood is arguably the most important part of any woodworking project; here are my tips on what to look for and how to store it.

PLANED PINE

Because this book is aimed primarily at people who are new to woodworking and the tools are mostly simple hand tools, I suggest you use a soft wood, such as pine, for most of the projects. Pine is cheaper to buy than hard wood, easier to work with, and readily available.

PLYWOOD (man-made boards)

Plywood is made from thin sheets of veneer that are laminated together to make one large, strong sheet. Each layer of veneer is glued at a right angle to the one below; it is the gluing and layering that makes it strong and durable. Because of its strength and the size of the sheets in which it can be purchased, plywood is the perfect material for the back panels of cupboards. Many hardware stores sell small off-cuts, so you don't have to go out and buy one big sheet. Always wear a mask when working with plywood.

MDF (medium-density fiberboard)

Available in different thicknesses, MDF is manufactured by mixing very fine wood fiber with a resin adhesive and then compressing it into large sheets. It has a fine, flat surface, which makes it good for painting on. Always wear a dust mask suitable for use with MDF.

FOLLOWING A CUTTING LIST

A cutting list gives you the exact measurements that you need to make the project; it shows you the number of panels required and enables you to label each panel. The measurements are listed in both imperial and metric; make sure you follow one system or the other, as sometimes there are very slight differences in the measurements between the two.

If you want to make life a little easier for yourself, take the cutting list to the hardware store and get them to cut the wood for you.

Buying and storing wood

* TRY TO CHOOSE THE WOOD YOURSELF, SO THAT YOU CAN MAKE SURE YOU PICK OUT THE BEST PIECES. IF YOU ARE NOT PERMITTED TO MOVE THE WOOD YOURSELF, ASK IF YOU CAN BE THERE TO INSPECT THE WOOD.

* ALWAYS TAKE A TAPE MEASURE AND THE MATERIALS OR CUTTING LIST FOR YOUR PROJECT WITH YOU TO BE SURE YOU BUY THE RIGHT TYPE AND AMOUNT OF WOOD.

* ALWAYS BUY EXTRA WOOD TO ALLOW FOR MISTAKES OR WORKING AROUND KNOTS. IN MOST OF THE PROJECTS IN THIS BOOK, I HAVE ALREADY ADDED ON THE EXTRA WOOD IN THE MATERIALS LIST.

* CHECK EACH PIECE OF WOOD FOR DEFECTS.

* STORE YOUR WOOD ON A FLAT SURFACE, AWAY FROM DIRECT SUNLIGHT AND HEAT SOURCES SUCH AS RADIATORS.

TECHNIQUES

Like any other craft or skill, there are some techniques that you need to know; all are relatively simple to master.

TRANSFERRING TEMPLATES TO CARDSTOCK

Transferring the template onto cardstock means that it will be more robust if you are going to use it more than once. The technique for doing this is very simple.

1 First, place tracing paper over the template and trace over the lines with a soft pencil.

2 Turn the tracing paper over and scribble over the lines on the back of the template.

3 Turn the template over again, place it on cardstock, and draw back over the lines on the tracing paper; the pencil marks that you scribbled on the reverse will transfer the lines onto the cardstock; now you can cut out the cardstock, place it on your wood, and draw around it to give you the lines you need to cut along.

An alternative is to use carbon paper; however, I prefer to use the tracing-paper method, as it means I can see what I'm doing.

Drawing around templates on your wood

✳ WHEN PLACING YOUR TEMPLATE ON THE WOOD, CONSIDER THE DIRECTION OF THE GRAIN: THE WOOD IS WEAKER ACROSS THE GRAIN AND STRONGER ALONG THE LENGTH OF THE GRAIN.

✳ AVOID KNOTS IN THE WOOD, UNLESS YOU DECIDE THAT THIS IS GOING TO BE PART OF THE CHARACTER OF YOUR DECORATION.

✳ PLACE YOUR TEMPLATE NEAR THE EDGE OF THE WOOD SO THAT YOU WILL HAVE LESS SAWING TO DO BEFORE YOU REACH YOUR TEMPLATE LINES.

✳ WHEN USING PLYWOOD, THE DIRECTION OF THE GRAIN IS NOT IMPORTANT: BECAUSE OF THE WAY PLYWOOD IS MADE, THERE IS NO WEAKNESS IN IT.

✳ IF YOU ARE USING TONGUE-AND-GROOVE PANELING, REMEMBER TO PLACE THE TEMPLATE AWAY FROM THE GROOVE.

DRILLING PILOT HOLES AND DRIVING IN SCREWS

A pilot hole is a small hole that you drill before driving a screw into a piece of wood. It prevents the screw from splitting the wood and it ensures that the screw will be installed straight, because it will follow the path of the pilot hole.

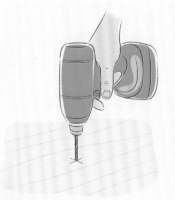

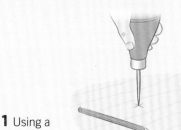

1 Using a pencil, mark on the wood where you want the screw to go. Make a small indentation in the wood using a bradawl. (For larger screws, you can use a center punch instead of a bradawl.) This will help stop the drill bit from slipping when you start the pilot hole.

2 Insert the appropriate bit into your drill: the bit for a pilot hole should be smaller than the diameter of the screw you're intending to use. (Remember that you can always make the pilot hole bigger if you need to.)

4 Fit your drill with a screwdriver bit. Place the tip of the screw in the pilot hole and drive the screw in, angling it so that it follows the path of the pilot hole.

3 Place the tip of the bit in the indentation you made in step 1, angling it at the angle you want the screw to follow, then drill the hole to a depth equal to the length of the screw. Back the bit out carefully.

COUNTERSINKING SCREWS

Countersinking screws simply means driving them in so that they sit flush with the surface of the wood. There is a special bit for doing this. The bit makes an indentation in the wood above your pilot hole, then the screw head fits snugly, flush with the membrane of the wood.

1 Drill a pilot hole for the screw (see page 127), using a drill bit about half the diameter of the screw you are intending you to use. If you are using a countersink bit (see page 125), simply locate the point of the countersink bit in the pre-drilled pilot hole and drill down a little way, creating a tapered recess. Place the head of the screw in the recess you've just made to check the size: the recess should be fractionally larger than the screw head. If you are using a hand-held countersink tool, place the point of the tool in the drilled hole, push down, and twist the handle round while pushing; this will scrape away the wood, leaving a tapered recess.

2 Insert the screw until the head is flush with the surface of the wood. Fill with wood filler putty, leave to dry, then sand the filler flush with the surface of the wood.

DOWEL JOINT

A dowel joint is for joining wood together. It can be used for corner joints or for laminating wood to make a wider panel. It is the easiest and cheapest way for somebody to start learning how to join wood. The method we are using for this joint is the center-point method. It is one of the first joints I learned—and my furniture is still standing so I know that, if it is done properly, it will make a very good piece of furniture.

For the dowel joint projects in this book, I have named the panels that you will be joining as either Panel 1 or Panel 2; label each panel as soon as it is mentioned in the instructions, so that you don't get confused.

Panel 1 will be the panel that you drill into first and into which you place the center-point markers. Panel 2 is the panel that will be pushed down onto the center-point markers, in the end grain, to mark where the dowels will go.

Make corresponding marks on the two panels as soon as you have marked out the joint, to make them easier to identify.

1 Following the relevant templates or project instructions, mark the position of the holes for the dowel joints on Panel 1.

2 Start working on Panel 1. Apply a masking-tape marker to the ¼-in. (6-mm) dowel drill bit at one-third of the length of the dowel and drill the holes for the dowel joints at the marked points. Sand away any break-out from the drilling.

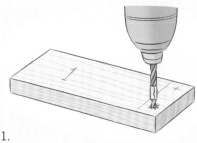

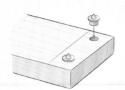

3 Place the center-point markers in the drilled holes on Panel 1. Push them all the way in. If it is too hard to push them down all the way with your finger, use the end of a flat-headed screwdriver to finish pushing them in.

YOU WILL NEED

Workbench

Clamps

Masking tape

Drill

Coarse to fine sandpaper

1 x ¼-in. (6-mm) dowel center-point marker kit

Flat-headed screwdriver

Pencil

Tri-square (optional)

¼-in. (6-mm) fluted dowels

Wood glue

Mallet

4 Place Panel 2 over the center-point markers in Panel 1, making sure that both edges are in the correct position. (Remember to mark each joint so that you can identify it later.) Push down hard, ensuring that the center-point markers mark the position of the dowel joints on Panel 2. Mark the holes with pencil.

✻ TO MAKE STEP 4 EASIER, CLAMP DOWN PANEL 1, PLACE A TRI-SQUARE UP TO THE EDGE AND SLOWLY LOWER PANEL 2 DOWN ONTO THE CENTER-POINT MARKERS. THEN PUSH DOWN HARD, ENSURING THAT THE POINTS MARK THE POSITION OF THE DOWEL JOINTS ON PANEL 2. (THE TRI-SQUARE KEEPS BOTH PANELS FLUSH.)

5 Remove the center point markers. You may need to lever them out with a flat-headed screwdriver.

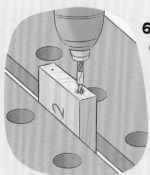

6 Clamp panel 2 into the workbench. On the ¼-in. (6-mm) drill bit, apply a masking-tape marker at just over two-thirds of the length of the dowel and drill the holes for the dowel joints. You will be drilling into the end grain.

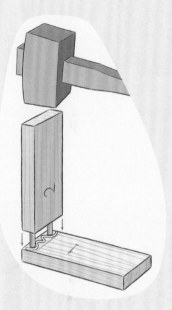

7 The gluing process needs to be done quickly. Place a small amount of glue in the dowel holes on Panel 1 and a small wiggly line along the surface. Insert a fluted dowel into each hole. Apply a small amount of glue into the dowel holes of Panel 2 and, using a mallet, tap down Panel 2 so that it sits firmly up against Panel 1. If the two panels are not closing together, place them in a clamp; for larger projects, use a sash clamp and tighten the clamp to bring them together.

LAMINATING WOOD

Laminating wood is a process of joining small boards of wood together to make one large panel. There are several ways of joining pieces of wood together, but for this book I will show you how to use the dowel center-point marker kit—the cheapest and easiest method for someone starting out for the first time in woodwork.

The method is the same as that for making dowel joints (see opposite)— it's the way in which you mark out your wood that is different. The wood in the material list is a manageable size for practicing on for the first time.

1 First, check that all the boards have a true square edge and the wood has no warping defects such as cupping, twisting, and bowing.

2 Place the four boards on the workbench side by side and look at the end grain of each one. The end grain you can see is the growth rings of the tree. For added stability and to reduce cupping of the panel, turn the boards so that the growth rings face in opposite directions on alternate boards. Check that the boards sit well together and then number each one so you know the order in which you have placed them.

YOU WILL NEED

Workbench

Four planed pine boards, 20 x 3¾ x ¾ in. (510 x 95 x 20 mm)

Pencil

Machinist or engineering square

Sash or bar clamps

Masking tape

Drill

Coarse to fine sandpaper

Dowel center-point marker kit (you will need four center-point markers)

Flat-headed screwdriver

Wood glue

¼-in. (6-mm) fluted dowels

Mallet

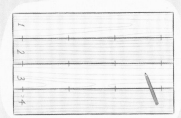

3 While you have all the boards in their correct positions on the workbench, mark the position of each dowel. To start with, place the markings on the top face of the boards. The two end dowels need to be about 2 in. (50 mm) from the end of the board; thereafter, depending on the length of the board, space the dowels evenly 4–7½ in. (100–190 mm) apart.

✳ FOR 20-IN. (510-MM) BOARDS, YOU WILL NEED FOUR DOWELS; FOR 40-IN. (1020-MM) BOARDS, I WOULD USE SIX DOWELS AND SPACE THEM ABOUT 7 IN. (180 MM) APART. THE SPACING DOES NOT NEED TO BE EXACT; IT WILL NOT WEAKEN YOUR BOARD IF THE END DOWELS HAVE TO BE A BIT FURTHER OR CLOSER TOGETHER THAN ALL THE OTHER DOWELS.

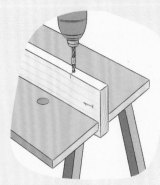

4 Using a machinist or engineering square, draw a line from each dowel mark on the first panel to halfway across the thickness. This will be the position for each dowel. Securely clamp the first panel into the workbench. Apply a masking-tape marker to the dowel drill bit at just over half the length of the dowel and drill each hole. Sand away any break-out from the drilling.

5 Place a center-point marker in each of the dowel holes and place the second board on top. Make sure the front faces and the ends of the boards are flush. Push the second board down onto the center-point markers. This will mark the second board, indicating where you will drill the holes for the dowels. Remove the center-point markers ready to re-use them on the next board; you can use a flat-headed screwdriver to ease them out.

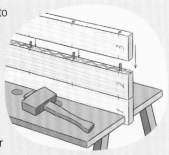

6 Repeat steps 4 and 5 to mark and drill the dowel holes for the other edge of the second board and place the third board in the same way to indicate where the holes will be drilled. Repeat for the third and fourth boards.

7 To glue the panel together, securely clamp the first board into the workbench. Apply glue into the dowel holes and place the dowels in position. Use a mallet to tap them in place. Making sure you work on the correct edge of the second board, apply a wiggly line of glue along the second board and into the dowel holes, then place the second board in position on the first board and push it down onto the dowels. Use a mallet to knock the two boards together as much as possible. Repeat for each board, building them up into a large panel.

✳ IF YOU NOTICE THE PANEL CUPPING AS YOU ARE CLAMPING, IT, UNDO THE SASH CLAMPS AND TURN THE PANEL OVER SO THAT THE CENTER OF THE PANEL IS RESTING ON THE BAR OF THE CLAMPS, THEN TIGHTEN THE CLAMPS JUST ENOUGH SO THEY ARE GRIPPING ONTO THE PANEL AND PUSH THE TWO OUTER EDGES OF THE PANEL DOWN SO THAT THE PANEL IS FLUSH WITH THE STRAIGHT BAR OF THE CLAMP. IF YOU HAVE A THIRD CLAMP, USE IT TO CLAMP ONTO THE OTHER SIDE OF THE PANEL; THIS HELPS TO BALANCE OUT THE PRESSURE APPLIED ON THE PANEL AND REDUCE CUPPING.

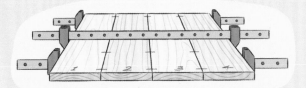

8 Working quickly, clamp the large panel of four boards into the sash clamps. The sash clamps will push the boards together and hold them until the glue has dried.

9 Wipe away any glue from both sides of the panel. Leave the clamped panel on a flat and even surface until the glue has dried.

DECORATIVE EFFECTS

Many of the projects in this book have had a decorative finish applied to them. Here are some simple techniques to try.

PAINTS AND VARNISHES

All the paints and varnishes used in these projects are water based, which means that there will be no harmful chemicals and the brushes can easily be rinsed out with warm water. Although there should not be any strong fumes, you should always work in a well-ventilated area. For projects that are going to be placed in the garden, you will need either exterior paint or a finish that will protect it from the weather.

Matte latex (emulsion) paint is a good, multi-purpose paint that works well on wood and is available in a vast range of colors. For small projects, buy tester pots of paint or ask friends for any of their tester pots that they don't need any more.

Satinwood paint is primarily for wood and metal. It is a tough and durable paint that can be easily wiped clean, making it perfect for projects that will get a lot of use. For painting on bare wood, always use a primer, which seals and gives a good base coat for the satinwood paint to adhere to. Undercoat is for painting over pre-painted surfaces; it helps to adhere the paint to the already painted surface, which helps stop the paint from flaking off.

For some projects I apply a **clear matt varnish** to protect the paintwork. If the project is for exterior use, I give it two coats of varnish with a light sanding in between. For interior items one coat of varnish will be enough. Always read the manufacturer's instructions before use.

SANDING PRIOR TO PAINTING

Sanding prior to painting not only removes any rough edges or splinters, it also provides a "key" for the paint, meaning that it will adhere more evenly.

1 Sand the piece with coarse sandpaper to remove any rough edges remaining from the sawing. Then use fine sandpaper all over until you have the finish and shape you require. Work with the grain.

2 Rub the piece with an old cloth to remove any dust.

BASIC PAINTING

Time and patience during the painting process will improve the quality of the finish. The more coats of paint you apply, the deeper the color you will achieve.

1 Lightly sand the item to remove any break-out or saw marks.

2 Using a medium flat brush, apply the first coat. Start by painting the edges and lightly brush over any build-up of paint as you go along. Once you have finished the edges, work on the rest of the piece, taking care to always paint with the grain.

YOU WILL NEED

Fine sandpaper
Water-based paint
Medium flat paintbrush
Heat gun (optional)

3 Leave to dry completely. To speed up the drying process, I use a heat gun—it takes just seconds to dry this way.

4 The painting process will have caused some of the wood fibers to rise, making it look and feel rough. To achieve a smooth finish, rub over the piece with fine sandpaper, again starting with the edges and then over the rest of the piece, until you are happy with the finish. Wipe over with an old cloth to remove any dust.

5 Repeat step 2 to apply a second coat. If you are happy with the finish, you may not need to sand after this coat; if you think it could do with more than two coats, sand lightly and then paint again.

POLKA DOTS

This technique may take some practicing, but once you have mastered it you can apply it to almost any of the projects in the book. Always use a round brush to create the dots. The size of the dots will depend on the size of the brush you use: the larger the brush, the larger the dot.

1 Paint the piece in your chosen base color, following the basic painting instructions on page 131, and leave to dry completely.

2 Place the piece on a clean, flat surface and lay the polka-dot stencil over the top, lining up the dots so that they are symmetrical. Using a pencil, mark where you want the dots to go.

YOU WILL NEED

Polka-dot stencil (available from craft stores)
Pencil with a blunt nib
Two colors of water-based paint
Medium round brush

3 Check the consistency of the paint; make sure it isn't too runny or the dots won't hold their shape.

4 Dip your brush into the paint until a drop of paint forms on the end of your brush. Very lightly touch one of the pencil marks and let the paint form a dot on the piece; as soon as you can see the dot forming, carefully lift the brush away—there should now be a slightly raised dot on the surface of the piece.

5 Leave to dry. Do not use a heat gun to dry the dots, as it will cause them to dry unevenly.

TO GET THE DOTS EVEN, DIP YOUR BRUSH IN THE PAINT EACH TIME YOU DO A DOT AND APPLY THE SAME AMOUNT OF PRESSURE WITH THE BRUSH. DO NOT PUSH YOUR BRUSH DOWN TOO HARD OR YOUR DOTS WILL BECOME MISSHAPEN.

YOU WILL NEED

Fine sandpaper
Water-based paint in two colors
Medium flat paintbrush
Heat gun (optional)
Latex-based glue

RUSTIC FINISH

This technique has been around for a long time and is very popular on painted furniture. It does take time to do because of the layers of paint you need to apply to get a good finish, but it is well worth it and is very rewarding.

1 Sand your piece ready for painting. Apply two coats of your chosen base color, remembering to sand lightly between coats. Leave to dry completely or use a heat gun.

2 Apply latex-based glue randomly around the edges of the piece and leave to dry completely. This creates a layer that can be rubbed away after the final paint finish, to reveal the base coat. You may choose to have only a few patches or to have large areas. It depends on how rustic-looking you want your piece to be.

3 Using the basic paint technique, paint the entire piece in your chosen top coat. Depending on the colors and the quality of the paint, you may need to apply two or more coats of paint. Leave to dry.

4 Using fine sandpaper, lightly rub over the edges of the piece to remove the top coat of paint and the dried latex-based glue, revealing the base color. Make sure that you work with the grain and don't sand too much as you will sand down to the wood.

DECOUPAGE TECHNIQUE

This is a lovely technique to learn: it's quick and easy to do and is great for using up odd pieces of decorative paper that you have lying around the house. Avoid sanding the edges of any item you wish to apply paper to, as it helps if they are kept crisp and sharp for applying the paper.

1 Paint your piece following the instructions for basic painting on page 131. There is no need to paint the whole piece—just the edges and a little paint along the outside edges of the two faces.

2 Cut a piece of decorative paper slightly larger than the surface you will be covering, taking the pattern on the paper into account. (For example, if there is a large motif, make sure it is centered on the piece; if you are using a striped paper, make sure that the stripe aligns with the center of the piece.)

3 Apply PVA glue evenly over the face you wish to cover.

4 Place the paper in position on the glued area and hold the piece up to the light; you should be able to see the piece through the paper. Slide the paper to where you would like the pattern to be positioned, then gently rub from the center out to the edges, making sure the paper is stuck down firmly. Leave to dry completely.

5 Trim off the paper as close to the edges as you can.

6 Gently sand the edges to remove any remaining paper.

ATTACHING ITEMS TO THE WALL

There is more than one way to attach things to a wall—it all depends on the size and weight of the item and what type of wall it is being attached to. There are also several types of fixing: the one you choose depends on the surface you are drilling into and how heavy the item is.

Before you drill into any wall, make sure you test the area with a multi-detector. This is a device that will locate where electric cables, water pipes, and studs are sited behind the plaster. It is worth investing in a good-quality one.

TYPES OF FIXING

Apart from self-drill plasterboard fixings, all these fixings need to be inserted into a pre-drilled hole. For drilling into brick and concrete, you will need a masonry drill bit. For drilling into plasterboard, I use a HSS (High Speed Steel) drill bit and then a masonry bit if necessary.

Wall plug

Made of plastic, these come in three weight-bearing strengths.
Use on: Plasterboard, brick, and concrete
Screw type: Wood screw

Plasterboard plug

Made of plastic, similar to the wall plug, these have an anchor that expands out and locks onto the back of the plasterboard.
Use on: Plasterboard
Screw type: Wood screw

Self-drill plasterboard fixing

These are the fixings I like the most—they are easy to use and you don't need to use a drill. Available in plastic or metal, you simply tap them in with a hammer so that the point penetrates the plasterboard and then use a cross-head (Phillips) screwdriver to screw them in.

Use on: Plasterboard
Screw type: Screws are normally supplied with the fixings

Thunderbolt (hex head) fixing

This is a steel fixing, perfect for projects such as the coat hooks on page 28 where there is a lot of weight to bear. No wall plugs are needed: just drill a hole straight into the wall, insert the thunderbolt, and tighten using a ratchet spanner. Refer to the packaging for details of what size of drill bit to use.

Use on: Concrete, brick, wood, and stone
Screw type: None required

HANGING FIXTURES

These are fixings that you need to attach to your cabinets, key hooks, and so on to mount them onto the wall.

Single/double D-rings

Used for light- and mediumweight frames, double D-rings being the strongest. The screws are normally very small, so use a bradawl to make a pilot hole (see page 122).

Glass/mirror plates

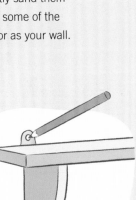

Used for mounting heavy mirror or picture frames, shelving, and small cupboards. They are easy to attach: simply space them out to distribute the weight evenly and use a bradawl to make a pilot hole (see page 122). If you do not want them to stand out and be visible, lightly sand them down with some fine sandpaper to remove some of the lacquer and then paint them the same color as your wall.

MOUNTING ONTO A WALL WITH GLASS/MIRROR PLATES

Using glass/mirror plates is an easy way of mounting items on a wall. The method shown here uses wall plugs; if you decide to use any of the other types of wall fixings, read through the advice on how to use them.

YOU WILL NEED

Multi-detector (for wires, pipes, and studs)
Pencil
Drill
Drill bit
Wall plugs (if necessary)
Glass/mirror plates
Hammer
Wood screws
Screwdriver
Spirit level

1 Using a multi-detector, check the wall for wires, pipes, and studs. Place the item in position on the wall and use a pencil to mark the position of one of the screw holes through the glass/mirror plate. Depending on the size and weight of the item, you may need someone to hold it in place while you mark. Remove the item.

2 Drill a hole at the marked point, using the correct size drill bit for the wall fixing you have chosen. Insert a wall plug into the hole.

3 Insert the wood screw through the hole of the hanging plate and locate the tip of the screw to the wall plug, then lightly screw the item to the wall.

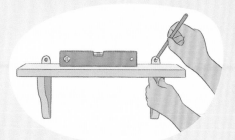

4 Use a spirit level to make sure that the item is level on the wall. Now mark the position for the second screw hole with a pencil, through the hanging plate. Remove the first screw and take the item down from the wall.

5 Drill the second screw hole and insert a wall plug.

6 Place the second screw in place through the hanging plate and lightly screw to the wall. Before tightening this screw, locate the other screw back through the hanging plate and into the wall plug and lightly screw to the wall. Once you are happy that the shelf is sitting straight, tighten the two screws so that the shelf is tightly secured to the wall.

MOUNTING STRAIGHT ONTO A WALL

Some projects, such as the coat hooks on page 28 and the tool hooks on page 79, need to be attached straight to the wall through the back panel.

YOU WILL NEED

Multi-detector (for wires, pipes, and studs)

Suitable wall fixings

Screwdriver or ratchet spanner

Drill

Drill bit

Wall plugs (if necessary)

Spirit level

Bradawl or long, thin nail

1 Using a multi-detector, check the wall for wires, pipes, and studs. Insert a screw or bolt in your item through one of the pre-drilled holes. (If you are using a thunderbolt fixing, the screw hole in the item needs to be slightly larger than the diameter of the thunderbolt.) Screw it in far enough for the tip of the screw to protrude out through the back.

2 Position your item on the wall and push hard, so that the tip of the screw marks the wall. Remove the item.

3 Drill the first screw hole in the wall, following Step 2 of the basic mounting instructions, and insert a wall plug (or leave clear if you are using a thunderbolt fixing).

4 Use a screwdriver (or ratchet spanner if you are using a thunderbolt fixing) to lightly screw the item to the wall.

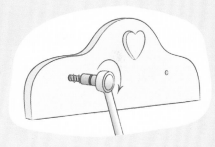

5 Use a spirit level to make sure the item is level on the wall.

6 If the holes in your item are big enough, use a bradawl to push through the remaining screw hole(s) and mark their position on the wall, ready for drilling. If the holes are too small for a bradawl, use a long, thin nail to mark the wall.

7 Unscrew the item from the wall, and then drill and plug the remaining hole(s).

8 Attach all the screws to your item and screw in until the tips of the screws protrude out through the back.

9 Locate the tips of the screws/bolts to the wall plugs or the drilled holes in the wall and screw tight to the wall.

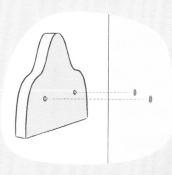

TEMPLATES

All the templates you need are provided here. The templates on pages 136–8 are full-size and can be traced, while the templates on pages 139–42 are half-size, and you will need to enlarge them by 200% to double them. Many domestic all-in-one printers have an option to copy and enlarge; alternatively, go to your local printers or stationery store and ask them to enlarge it for you.

   Some templates have a "place to fold" mark, meaning you need to place them on a folded piece of paper and cut them out to get the whole shape.

   The crosses on the templates indicate where you will need to make screw holes.

GARDEN-PARTY BUNTING

(page 98)

Full-size template

WINGED ANGEL

(page 95)

Full-size templates

CUPCAKE GARLAND

(page 92)

Full-size template

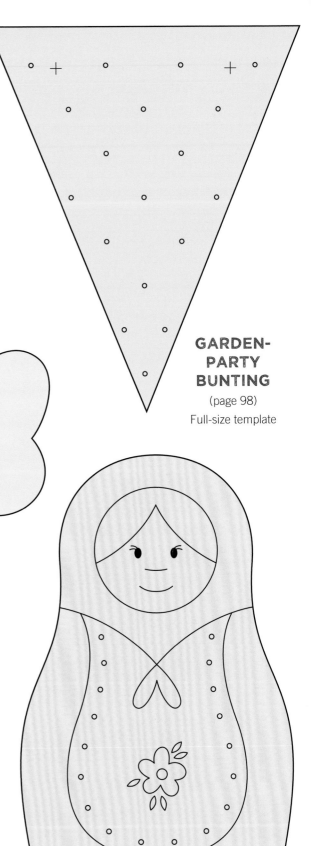

MATRYOSHKA BOOKENDS

(page 19)

Full-size template

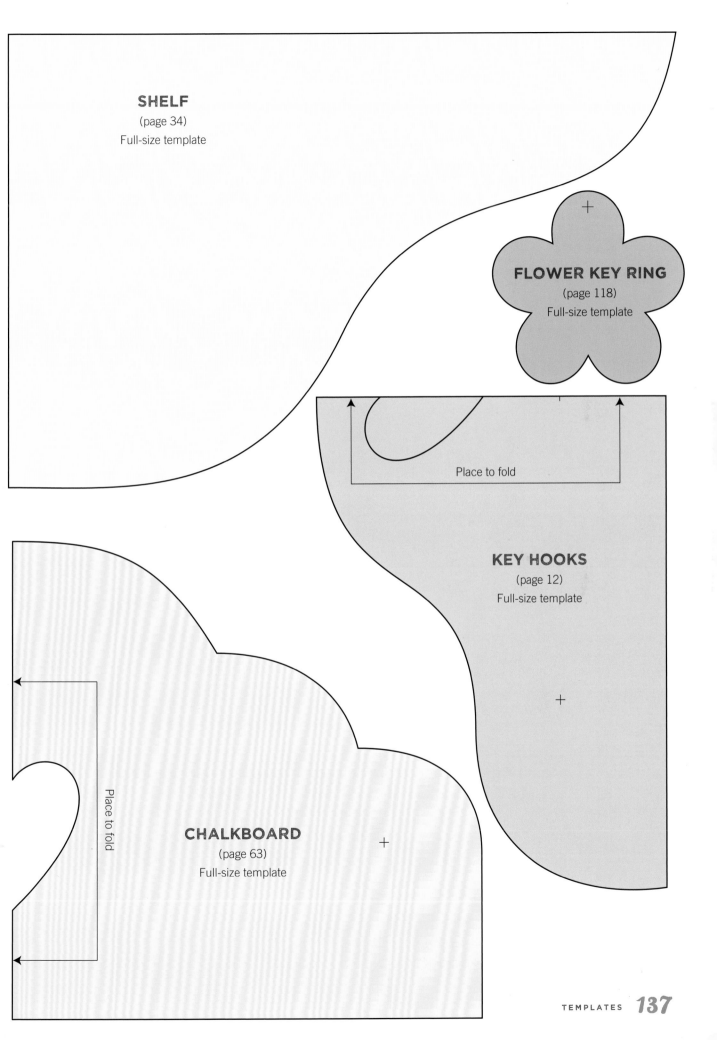

SHELF
(page 34)
Full-size template

FLOWER KEY RING
(page 118)
Full-size template

Place to fold

KEY HOOKS
(page 12)
Full-size template

Place to fold

CHALKBOARD
(page 63)
Full-size template

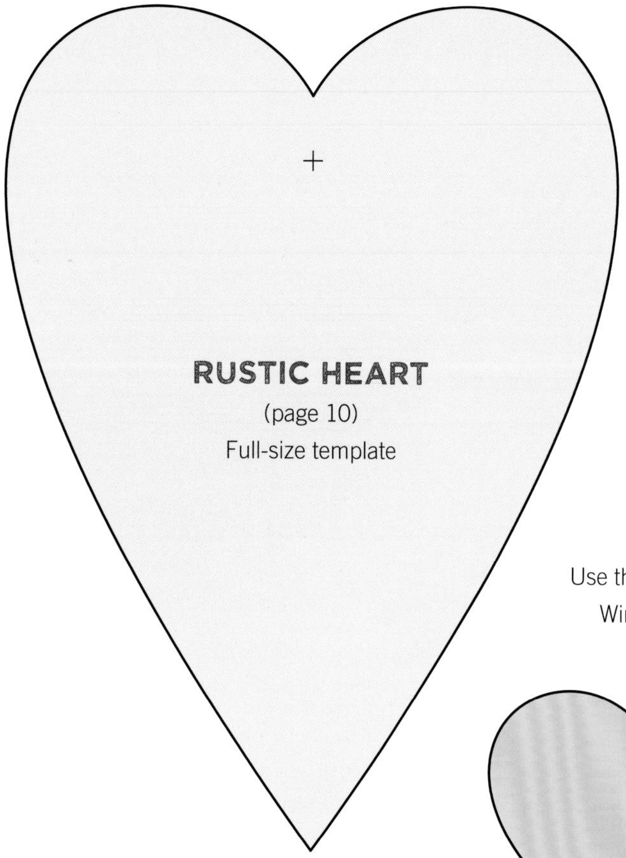

RUSTIC HEART
(page 10)
Full-size template

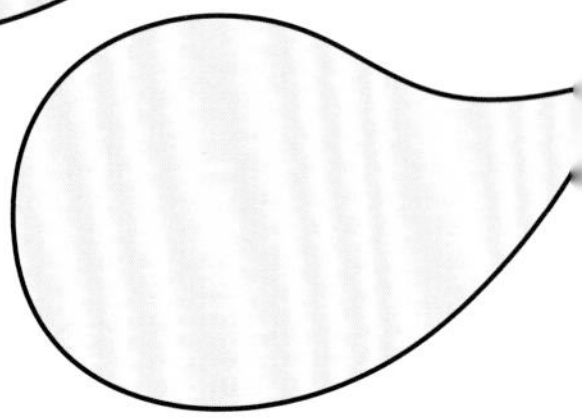

BIRD WITH FABRIC WINGS
(page 14)
Full-size templates

RUSTIC BIRD
(page 10)
Use the bird template for the Bird with Fabric
Wings, but use only the top screw hole.

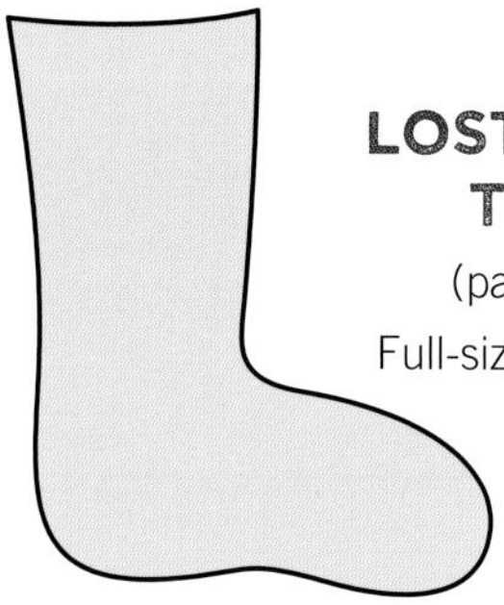

LOST SOCK TIDY
(page 56)
Full-size template

CUPCAKE GARLAND AND PAINTED NECKLACE
(pages 92 and 110)
Full-size template

FREESTANDING HEART
(page 107)
Full-size template

HOME IS WHERE THE HEART IS
(page 104)
Full-size templates

STORAGE BOX
(page 74)
Half-size template

HANGING MOON
(page 26)
Half-size template

SHOPPING PAD
(page 82)
Half-size template

FIVE-PLANK STOOL
(page 66)
Half-size templates

Dowel joint

Screw support

Dowel joint

TOWEL RAIL
(page 44)
Half-size templates

Place to fold

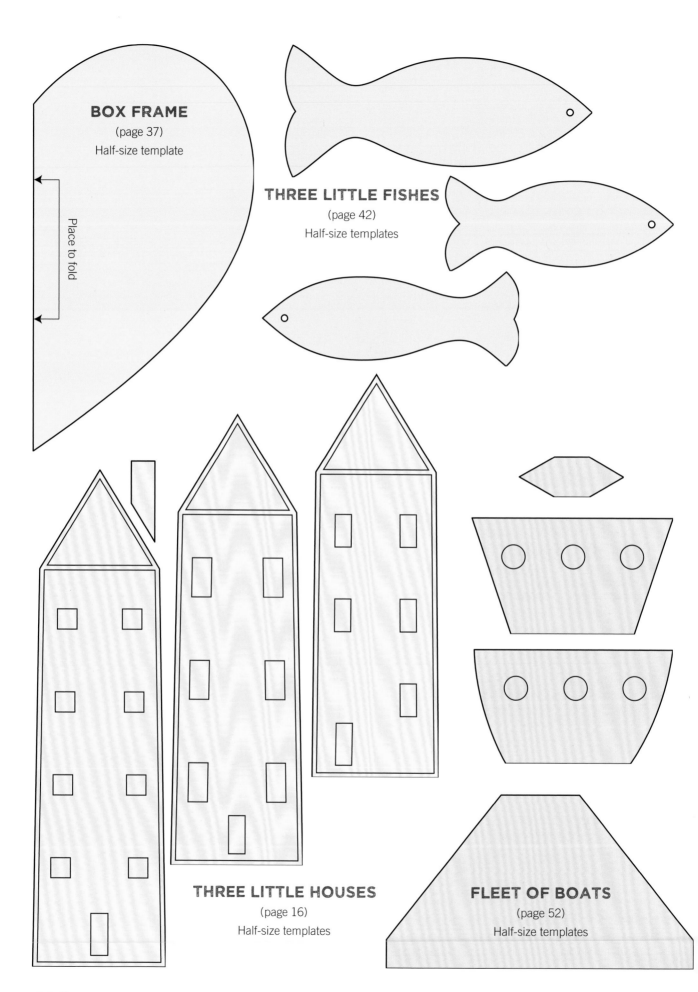

BOX FRAME

(page 37)

Half-size template

Place to fold

THREE LITTLE FISHES

(page 42)

Half-size templates

THREE LITTLE HOUSES

(page 16)

Half-size templates

FLEET OF BOATS

(page 52)

Half-size templates

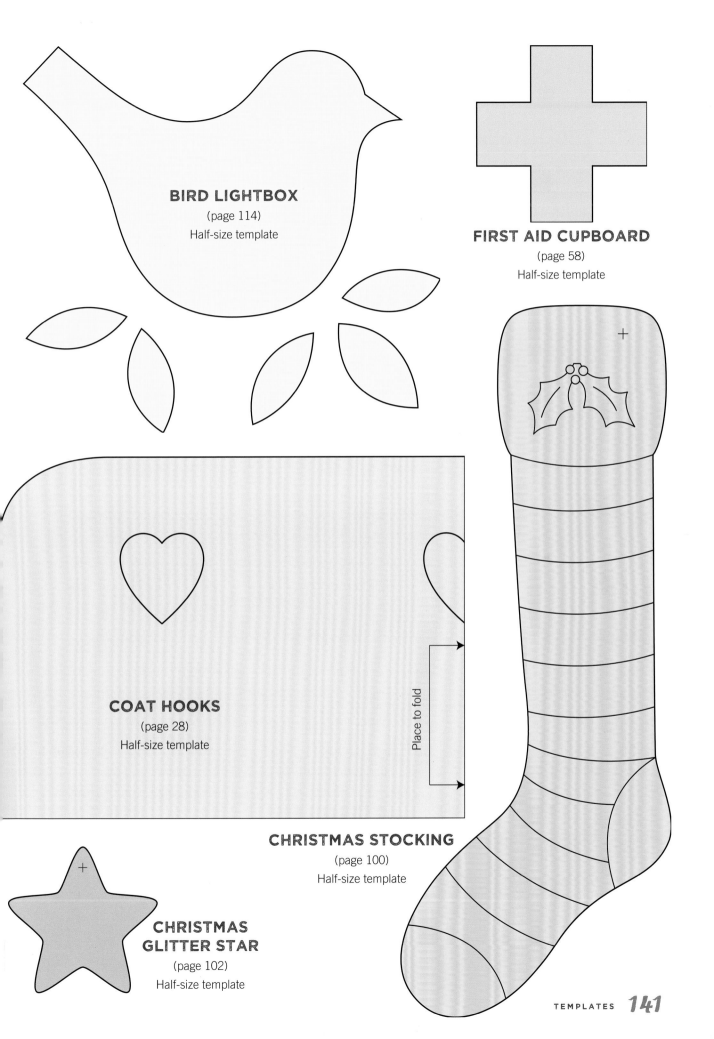

BIRD LIGHTBOX
(page 114)
Half-size template

FIRST AID CUPBOARD
(page 58)
Half-size template

COAT HOOKS
(page 28)
Half-size template

Place to fold

CHRISTMAS STOCKING
(page 100)
Half-size template

CHRISTMAS GLITTER STAR
(page 102)
Half-size template

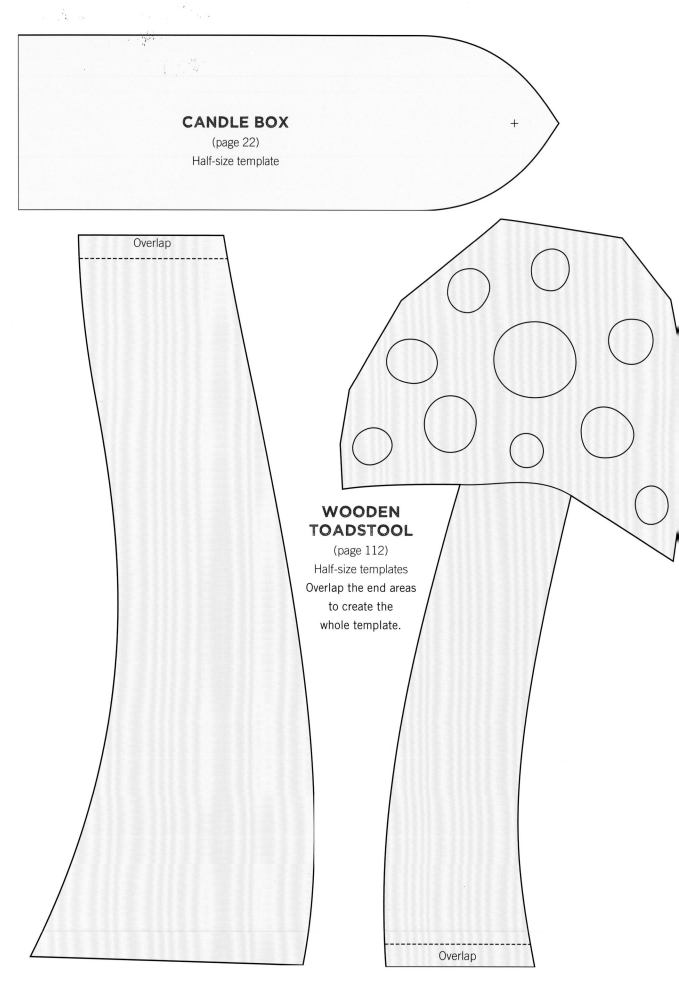

CANDLE BOX

(page 22)

Half-size template

+

Overlap

WOODEN TOADSTOOL

(page 112)

Half-size templates
Overlap the end areas
to create the
whole template.

Overlap

SUPPLIERS

HOME-IMPROVEMENT STORES AND HARDWARE STORES

The following are good sources of tools and hardware.

US

Ace Hardware www.acehardware.com 1-866-290-5334

The Home Depot www.homedepot.com 1-800-466-3337

Lowes www.lowes.com 1-800-445-6937

UK

Alex Wilkins Blacksmiths www.alexwilkinsblacksmiths.com 01531 670957

B&Q www.diy.com 0845 609 6688

Homebase www.homebase.co.uk 0845 077 8888

Wickes www.wickes.co.uk 0370 218 7683

CRAFT AND HOMEWARE STORES

These stores provide general crafting equipment for adding decoration to your projects.

US

Create For Less www.createforless.com 1-866-333-4463

Michael's www.michaels.com 1-800-642-4235

Save on Crafts www.save-on-crafts.com 1-831-768-8428

UK

Cath Kidston www.cathkidston.co.uk 0845 026 2440

Craft Superstore www.craftsuperstore.co.uk 0845 409 7595

Hobbycraft www.hobbycraft.co.uk 01202 596100

Homecrafts Direct www.homecrafts.co.uk 01162 697733

INDEX

ACKNOWLEDGMENTS

Jennifer Burt

My first thanks are to Joanna Teague for believing in me and in the things I love making, and for her support from writing that first book proposal to the hours spent together in my studio working through the instructions for each project.

Thanks to Trevor Steger for putting up with me over the years and letting me share his workshop and all the machines. Trevor is a true master craftsman, making some of the best furniture, doors, windows... The list goes on; there is nothing he can't make and I have learned so much from watching and listening to him. I feel so privileged to have met him and all his family.

Fiona has a lovely little shop called Three Little Pigs in Pershore and it is from supplying Fiona's shop that I really started to blossom and enjoy designing. It has been her support and encouragement over the years that have helped me to be where I am today. So a big thank you to you, your shop, and all your customers.

A special thanks to Cindy and Penny for giving me the opportunity to write this book. What you see here may be based on my designs and knowledge, but this is not my book alone: CICO have a very talented team whom I respect and admire very much and this book is a showcase for all that talent. To Sarah for her understanding of technical writing and adding clarity to the instructions; thank you for all your support as well. Thank you to Carmel; this has been made so much easier with your guidance and help. Thanks to Caroline and Nel for your amazing photography and styling, which have helped bring this book to life. And thank you to Steve for the wonderful illustrations.

Thank you to my husband, Simon, for supporting me through college and taking over the cooking while I have been busy designing and making, and to my children. I love you very much—all three of you make me very proud to be your mum.

Thank you to all my family and friends who have supported me and put up with me endlessly talking about my work. I love you all.

Joanna Teague

My thanks to my mum for having the things ready to make, to Jon for giving me time to make, to my kids for inspiring me to make, and to Jen for giving me the chance to write about making.